Amy Dillwyn

DAVID PAINTING

E. A. Dillwyn

To Joan, who made it possible

www.uwp.co.uk

British Library Cataloguing-in-Publication Data
A catalogue record for this book is available from the British Library.

ISBN   978-0-7083-2672-5
eISBN   978-0-7083-2679-4

Printed by CPI Antony Rowe, Chippenham

Contents

Foreword to the New Edition

This slim volume was first published twenty-five years ago, in 1987. In those days there were still a few people who fondly remembered 'Miss Dillwyn' as a Swansea 'character': a formidable elderly lady who wore mannish clothes and delighted in smoking a cigar. David Painting's research and deft penmanship revealed a far more remarkable individual and secured for Amy Dillwyn – industrialist, feminist, educationalist, activist and writer – a place in history. Indeed, this landmark study underpinned and informed all subsequent Amy Dillwyn scholarship to the present day, including my own; one might even go so far as to say that, without it, there might not have been any such scholarship at all.

Amy Dillwyn was born in 1845 and grew up with the privileges and constraints of a Victorian lady, a role she found increasingly difficult. An intelligent and energetic young woman, she spent her twenties increasingly despairing of finding a useful and fulfilling role in life. Debilitated in her late twenties by illness and depressed by personal frustrations, including unrequited love for her friend Olive Talbot, she took to writing first allegories, then novels and for over a decade strident reviews for *The Spectator*. But it was the loss of her beloved home on the death of her father in 1892 that proved a turning point in her life. In cheap lodgings, fighting a corrupt solicitor and coming to terms with her father's enormous debts, Amy Dillwyn found a new lease of life. Refusing to allow the family name to be associated with failure, she decided to take on a near-bankrupt spelter works, and after several years of hard work she was able to pay off the creditors and become the rightful owner of Dillwyn & Co. Her fluency in French and German, her self-taught arithmetic and her experience of running Hendrefoilan Home Farm all stood her in good stead for her new career as an industrialist. Although she employed a trusted manager, she was deeply involved in the business. In 1905, aged 60, she travelled in the depths of winter to the Atlas mountains in Algeria, to find a good source of calamine for her works. Inspecting mines and travelling by donkey into the snowy mountains, she was clearly a canny negotiator with an astute sense for business. When she regretfully sold her controlling shares in Dillwyn & Co. in 1906, it was done in the best interests of the company, but her will shows that she made her own fortune from the business she had saved from collapse. Already a prominent figure, Dillwyn would pursue public and campaigning roles for another twenty years, into her eighties.

Amy Dillwyn was dismissive of her career as a novelist, yet her writing has received considerable attention in recent years and she is undoubtedly one of the most important English-language writers from Wales in the nineteenth century. Since this biography was first published, Amy Dillwyn's long out-of-print novels have been 'rediscovered' by a new audience. In 2001, Dillwyn's first novel, *The Rebecca Rioter*, was reissued by Honno. It was an instant hit and has been through several editions since, making it one of the Honno Classics series' best-selling titles. First published to critical acclaim in 1880, *The Rebecca Rioter* marked the emergence of a new, politicised and feminist literature from Wales in the English language. An innovative novel and an important example of a cross-gender narrative (the story is told in the first-person by a Welsh-speaking working-class man who is radicalised by the Rebecca movement), it interweaves a feminist agenda, satirical critique of class privilege and social injustice, and a quasi-autobiographical romance. Intellectuals in nineteenth-century Russia certainly picked up on the political message, and *The Rebecca Rioter* was instantly translated into Russian and published in the radical journal *Otechestvennye zapiski* (Notes of the Fatherland) in the same year it first appeared in London.[1]

This biography helps us to understand how and why Amy Dillwyn came to write such an innovative novel, and particularly to understand the significance of wider family influences. David Painting is an authority on the Quaker antecedents of the Dillwyn family, and he explains the importance of Amy Dillwyn's Quaker-influenced upbringing. We grow to understand and sympathise with a tomboyish girl, whose passionate love of the outdoor freedoms afforded by the moors and coastline of Gower (even as she is seduced by the glamour and glitter of a royal drawing room) would later be put to service in her literature. Liberal politics were a lifelong concern of Amy Dillwyn, something she inherited from her father, Lewis Llewelyn Dillwyn, the well-known radical liberal MP, champion of Welsh disestablishment and eventually a supporter of Cymru Fydd (the home-rule movement in Wales). He was also directly involved in the events Dillwyn would fictionalise in her

---

1   See Bohata and Lovatt (2012). Amy Dillwyn's second novel, *Chloe Arguelle* (1881), was a satire on class privilege and was translated and published in the same magazine as *Lozh'* (The Lie) in 1882.

novel, as one of the magistrates who ambushed the Rebecca Rioters at Pontarddulais in 1843, and his personal account clearly provided inspiration for Dillwyn's novel. There is also insight into Dillwyn's ardent desire to be of use to the world, a conviction that drove her to establish her own literacy classes for local girls even as she had grave misgivings about her skills as an instructor. In this pen portrait, we grow to appreciate and admire Dillwyn's mischievous sense of adventure, her iconoclastic challenges to convention and authority, her concern for the disadvantaged, her impatience and outspokenness in the face of injustice or incompetence. And we are given a glimpse of her wry self-deprecating humour, which enlivens her fiction and, in her private diaries, prevents descent into self-pity in the face of a long illness.

In 2004, Amy Dillwyn was granted a place in the *Dictionary of National Biography*, joining three other members of her family (all male). And, in 2009, a second novel – Dillwyn's third – was published by Honno Classics: *A Burglary; or, Unconscious Influence*, edited by the French academic Alison Favre. A further novel, *Jill*, will be published in 2013, making Dillwyn the best represented author in the Honno Classics series to date. Increased public awareness has been matched by increased academic interest in Dillwyn's creative and industrial work. As new research bears fruit, there will of course be more stories to tell about Amy Dillwyn, new approaches to her fiction, and further assessment of her industrial, civic and feminist activities. But David Painting's biography remains the undisputed touchstone for readers trying to understand the significance of Dillwyn's wider family network – she came from a family of eminent scientists as well as politicians and industrialists – and, crucially, her remarkable career as a self-made businesswoman in what was very much a man's world. To have woven such an engaging and coherent narrative of a life that spanned ninety years – from the early Victorian period to the eve of the Second World War, from young debutante to shrewd middle-aged director of Dillwyn & Co, to activist, campaigner, fundraiser and minor celebrity in old age – is a remarkable achievement.

The welcome decision of University of Wales Press to reissue this book – with enhanced photographs and a new cover, but otherwise just as it appeared in 1987 – testifies both to its enduring relevance as a piece of original research and to the growing significance of its subject in the years since this book first brought Amy Dillwyn back into the public consciousness.

Kirsti Bohata
Swansea, November 2012

Preface to the New Edition

When my brief biography of Amy Dillwyn was first published in 1987, I had no idea she would be of continuing interest to a new generation of readers twenty-five years later. But I would like to think that this account of a brave, gifted woman who defied and defeated every kind of prejudice will still seem relevant when presented in a fresh format retaining the original unaltered text.

Times and attitudes have changed in the intervening years, and Kirsti Bohata's new introduction carries Amy's story forward into the twenty-first century. The introduction takes the earlier narrative into previously unexplored territory and places Amy in the larger context of Anglo-Welsh literary criticism, against the background of the campaign for women's equality and the desire for social justice.

Since Amy's diaries – generously entrusted to me by her great-niece, the late Mrs Olga Welbourn – cover only a small part of her ninety-year lifespan, there was much to learn from other sources, and I hope the result provides a firm base for further research as well as remaining accessible to the ordinary reader in search of a good story.

Amy's life fascinated me when I first encountered her diaries, and I hope it will continue to resonate with a whole new readership and perhaps even stir the memories of those who first met her in the pages of this book when she was virtually unknown. Before the biography appeared there were only dim recollections of an eccentric Grand Old Lady of Swansea; now there is a greater awareness of Amy Dillwyn's real personality and a far wider recognition of her exceptional achievement as a true pioneer in so many fields of human endeavour.

David Painting
December, 2012

Introduction

This is the story of an exceptional woman. Amy Dillwyn was born into one of Glamorgan's leading families in 1845 and died in Swansea in 1935. She is still well remembered by many people in the city as a formidable, rather eccentric old lady who prided herself on her independent and unorthodox views and dared to smoke large cigars in a period when women were reluctant even to smoke cigarettes in public. For those who still recall 'Miss Dillwyn' she was above all else a character, a 'grand old lady' from the mid-Victorian age, who lived on almost to the outbreak of the Second World War, a ninety-year-old marvel.

It is, however, worth delving a little deeper and looking at Amy Dillwyn as she was in her prime, for there emerges a far more interesting figure than the trilby-hatted, cigar-smoking individualist of popular memory. She was brave, highly intelligent, and a prototype feminist whose seemingly masculine attitudes were a lifelong protest against the suppression and exploitation of women of every class. Her diaries and family letters from the period in which she was most active socially offer a clear insight into her mind, and occasionally a discreetly veiled glimpse into her heart. That she had outstanding ability was always obvious from her public work, but it was only to her diaries that she confided her innermost thoughts. The conflicts and self-doubts with which she struggled as she sought to find a satisfying and rewarding role in life are as relevant for many women today as they were for her over a hundred years ago. Her success as a Welsh industrialist was as astonishing as it was unique.

Her diaries, seven leather-bound volumes in her firm legible hand, afford the modern reader a rare opportunity of looking directly into the life of an affluent Victorian lady whose family background and connections coupled with her sparkling intellect could hardly fail to make her a fascinating and significant character in the social history of south Wales.

Acknowledgements

I am particularly grateful for the generous help given by Amy Dillwyn's great-niece Olga Welbourn, by Richard Morris and by Sir Clive Edwards; also by Dr John Alban, Cynthia Colquitt-Craven, Stanley Croot, Rowley Davies, Arthur Hill, Murray McLaggan, Hugh Morgan, Vanda Morton, Gertrude Nicholl, Olive Nicholl, Hilary Thomas and Malcolm Thomas of the Society of Friends. For their photographic expertise I am indebted to my colleagues Roger Davies and (especially) Bill Pring. I would like to acknowledge the generous assistance of Richard Morris with the illustrations appearing in the book.

Selected Reading

Amy Dillwyn's Novels

The Rebecca Rioter: A Story of Killay Life (London: Macmillan, 1880; reissued Dinas Powys: Honno, 2001).

Chloe Arguelle (London: Tinsley Bros, 1881).

A Burglary; or, Unconscious Influence (London: Tinsley Bros, 1883; reissued Dinas Powys: Honno, 2009).

Jill (London: Macmillan, 1884; reissued Dinas Powys: Honno, 2013).

Nant Olchfa (a novel part-serialised in *The Red Dragon: The National Magazine of Wales*, vols X–XI, 1886–7).

Jill & Jack (London: Macmillan, 1887).

Maggie Steele's Diary (London: Cassell & Co., 1892).

Further Reading and Recent Criticism

Jane Aaron, *Nineteenth-Century Women's Writing from Wales: Nation, Gender and Identity* (Cardiff: University of Wales Press), pp. 129–31.

Kirsti Bohata and Steven Lovatt, 'The Russian Rioter: Amy Dillwyn's *The Rebecca Rioter* in *Otechestvennye zapiski*', in Katie Gramich (ed,), *Almanac: A Yearbook of Welsh Writing in English: Critical Essays*, vol. 16 (2012), 1–30.

Alison Favre, 'Introduction' to Amy Dillwyn, *A Burglary; or, Unconscious Influence* (Dinas Powys: Honno, 2009), pp. vii–xix.

Katie Gramich, 'Introduction' to Amy Dillwyn, *The Rebecca Rioter: A Story of Killay Life* (Dinas Powys: Honno, 2001), pp. v–xxi.

Tomos Owen, '"Never Again Stop the Way of a Welshman": Rioting and Rebellion in Amy Dillwyn's *The Rebecca Rioter*', in David Bell and Gerald Porter (eds), *Riots in Literature* (Newcastle: Cambridge Scholars Publishing, 2008), pp. 51–74.

Royal Prologue

In the middle of January 1863 Queen Victoria, still in deep mourning after the death of her beloved Prince Consort, sat down at Osborne to write to her dearest daughter Vicky, Princess Royal of England and Crown Princess of Prussia, at the Imperial Palace in Berlin. The Prince of Wales was shortly to be married to Princess Alexandra of Denmark and the poor Queen, quite unable to face the festivities, was determined to devolve some of her more onerous duties upon her children:

> Now let me say what I am anxious you should do about coming here for Bertie's marriage. I wish you, as our eldest daughter, to hold a Drawing-room for me at the end of February – either 26th or 28th – so I wish you to arrive on the 24th. Then I wish you to do the honours for me in the house during those two or three busy (to me dreadful) days.

The imperious tone of the command would hardly seem appropriate in a letter addressed to a Crown Princess who was already the proud mother of the future Kaiser Wilhelm II of Germany. The Queen, however, was accustomed to being obeyed, and so the dutiful Vicky at once consented to come to England to act on behalf of her prostrated mother. Thus the arrangements for the drawing-room were set in motion.

On the appointed day, Saturday 28 February, the ancient Palace of St James was filled to overflowing, with the cream of English society assembled to witness the 'coming out' of 250 young women who were to be presented at Court as an essential prerequisite to their taking their proper place in one of the most hierarchical societies in the civilized world. Her Royal Highness the Princess Victoria arrived punctually at 2 p.m. accompanied by her younger sister Princess Helena, soon followed by her brother Albert Edward, Prince of Wales, and his equerries. Since the heir to the throne was due to be married within a few days this was his last public appearance as England's most eligible bachelor, and a ceremony that was always splendidly impressive was thus also filled with a special romantic excitement calculated to stir the emotions of all the privileged girls for whom this day was never to be forgotten.

Resplendent in swaying crinolines and brilliant jewellery, mothers and daughters crammed the notoriously inadequate corridors of St James's Palace as they waited for the supreme moment when the debutantes were announced by the Lord Chamberlain and presented to the Royal family. Among them was a seventeen-year-old girl from Swansea who had just travelled up from south Wales for what was easily the most awe-inspiring event in her young life. After it was all over and she had retreated to the sabbath tranquillity of her elegant London home in Knightsbridge she sat down and gave her elder sister a full account of her experience:

> I am at last fairly launched into the world. I have paid my respects to high and mighty majesty represented by a stumpy little Princess Royal. Poor little dear, she must have been tired by the time she had done with her mother's loyal subjects yesterday. I let down my train at the right moment, sailed up the room, came on the royal trio considerably before I expected (partly because they were all so short that I could hardly see down so low) made my three profound curtseys and immediately had my train put over my arm again without any walking backwards at all. One thing we all thought odd was that while both the Princesses curtseyed in return for our doing ditto the Prince of Wales took not the least notice of our salutations. Everyone agreed that the Princess Royal looked very well and did the honours delightfully. The whole affair was capitally arranged; no crowding, no tearing of clothes, no squashing of crinolines, in short no inconvenience of any kind.

The girl's name was Amy Dillwyn; her father was Lewis Dillwyn, the widely respected Liberal MP for Swansea, and she was being launched by her family on the first stage of a journey intended to lead to marriage, motherhood and the strictly conventional life of a very wealthy Victorian lady. Her prospective husband, the only son of a prosperous industrialist, had been marked out for her since childhood by their respective fathers and her future seemed as financially and socially secure as anyone could hope for. But within a year of her presentation at Court and just as her hopes and expectations were about to come to fruition, a cruel fate intervened and her fiancé suddenly died.

The story has never been told of how Amy the debutante with the world at her feet evolved into 'Miss Dillwyn' the Swansea character once described as one of the most original women of the age. The tale of a Victorian girl's love affair and its aftermath opens up a newly discovered window into a world that has totally disappeared and reveals an extraordinary woman of exceptional spirit and personality of whom the modern feminist movement could be proud. There are many facets to Amy's unique personality, and her private letters and diaries enable her to speak for herself with the authentic voice of a Victorian who may not have been eminent but who was eminently memorable.

Family Background

Amy Dillwyn's exceptional strength of character, even at the early age of seventeen, derived from her distinguished ancestry and from her unconventional upbringing in Swansea. Her paternal great-grandfather was William Dillwyn the eminent American Quaker who, having grown up in West Virginia in a family that had emigrated from Herefordshire in the seventeenth century, returned to England after the War of Independence and settled in Hackney as a thriving businessman. William Dillwyn had been one of Thomas Clarkson's closest allies in the struggle to abolish the slave trade and was renowned on both sides of the Atlantic for his liberal and humanitarian views. His son and heir Lewis Weston Dillwyn (Amy's grandfather) was born in Hackney in 1778, went to a Quaker school in Tottenham, and was apprenticed by his father to the linen trade first in Dover and later in the city of London. Lewis Dillwyn from an early age devoted all his spare time to botany and conchology, and by the time he was in his early twenties he was already well known in scientific circles as the author of several important books in his chosen field. Had he not been a Quaker and therefore subject to all kinds of disabilities he would no doubt have gone to Oxford or Cambridge and carved out a career in scientific research.

However, his father insisted that Lewis, despite his scholarly preoccupations, should enter the world of commerce in which so many Quakers flourished and earn his living as a draper's assistant until such time as he could set up in business on his own behalf. While working in his father's linen warehouse at Corbet Court in Gracechurch Street the lively young Lewis, who still wore the distinctive broad-brimmed Quaker hat, met and fell in love with a girl named Mary Adams who was also known as Mary Llewelyn. Mary Adams was the natural daughter of a wealthy Glamorgan landowner, Colonel John Llewelyn, whose extensive properties made him one of the most influential men in south Wales. Since he had no legitimate children Colonel Llewelyn decided to leave his estate to Mary provided that she married and had offspring. To ensure her future Colonel Llewelyn paid for an expensive education for his natural child and saw to it that she grew up in a style of life befitting an heiress.

Whether Lewis Dillwyn knew that his sweetheart was to inherit a substantial fortune remains a matter for speculation, but it seems more than a coincidence that in 1802 his father invested over £12,000 in buying the Cambrian Pottery in Swansea and installed Lewis as manager. Since Lewis knew little of the technical skill involved in pottery manufacture and was far more interested in his botanical work on British confervae his father shrewdly retained the services of the previous owner George Haynes, thus allowing Lewis freedom to pursue his studies in botany and zoology. For the first few years after acquiring the pottery Lewis appears to have spent as much time in London as he did in Swansea and, as a result of his published research, he became a Fellow of the Royal Society in 1804 and of the Linnean Society two years later. By 1807 he had established himself sufficiently firmly both as scientist and businessman to ask Mary Adams to marry him, which she duly did at St James's, Piccadilly on 2 July 1807 after a long courtship.

Since Mary did not share his Quaker background Lewis Dillwyn took a step of considerable consequence in 'marrying out' of the Society of Friends and severing his formal connection with a faith that would have disqualified both him and his children from playing a full part in public life in that period. Ten years later when Colonel John Llewelyn died the south Wales estates of Penllergaer and Ynys-y-gerwyn passed to Lewis as principal trustee for his and Mary's eldest son, John Dillwyn. He would have found it difficult to manage his affairs if he had still been a practising Quaker, so he quietly abandoned his old persuasion and formally embraced the Established Church to which most of the landed gentry belonged. One of the few clues to his heart-searching on this delicate matter lies in his regularly bemoaning the agonizing tedium of having to endure long Anglican sermons after having been brought up in the practice of silent witness.

When Colonel Llewelyn's will was read in 1817 and it emerged that he had left his fortune to Mary's son there was a flood of litigation by various disgruntled members of the family who had fully expected the Penllergaer estates to revert to them. But Lewis Dillwyn, with his Quaker's head for business and a streak of ruthless ambition for his children, succeeded in warding off all the attacks on his son's precious inheritance and within a few years had secured his family's hold on some of the most valuable properties in south Wales.

Unfortunately, as Lewis Dillwyn foresaw, one long-term result of the prolonged legal wrangling over Penllergaer was a substantial imbalance between the solidly based wealth that accrued to his elder son John and the relatively slender financial provision made for his other children, especially for his second son Lewis Llewelyn Dillwyn (Amy's father). John (who added

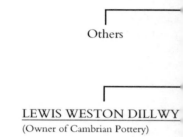

WILLIAM DILL'
(A Tottenham quaker w|

JOHN DILLWYN 1693–1

Others

LEWIS WESTON DILLWY
(Owner of Cambrian Pottery)

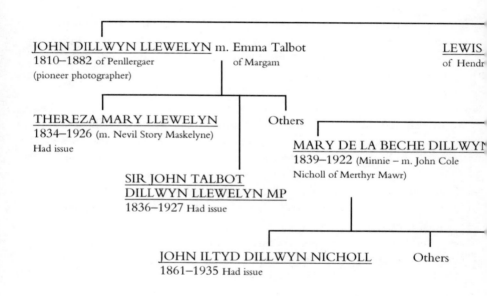

JOHN DILLWYN LLEWELYN m. Emma Talbot
1810–1882 of Penllergaer   of Margam
(pioneer photographer)

LEWIS
of Hendr

THEREZA MARY LLEWELYN
1834–1926 (m. Nevil Story Maskelyne)
Had issue

Others

MARY DE LA BECHE DILLWYI
1839–1922 (Minnie – m. John Cole
Nicholl of Merthyr Mawr)

SIR JOHN TALBOT
DILLWYN LLEWELYN MP
1836–1927 Had issue

JOHN ILTYD DILLWYN NICHOLL
1861–1935 Had issue

Others

Other

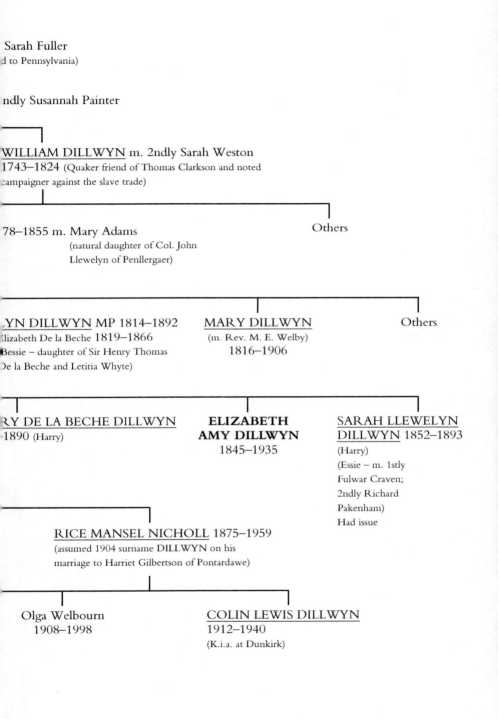

Sarah Fuller
d to Pennsylvania)

ndly Susannah Painter

WILLIAM DILLWYN m. 2ndly Sarah Weston
1743–1824 (Quaker friend of Thomas Clarkson and noted
campaigner against the slave trade)

78–1855 m. Mary Adams   Others
            (natural daughter of Col. John
            Llewelyn of Penllergaer)

YN DILLWYN MP 1814–1892   MARY DILLWYN   Others
lizabeth De la Beche 1819–1866   (m. Rev. M. E. Welby)
Bessie – daughter of Sir Henry Thomas   1816–1906
De la Beche and Letitia Whyte)

RY DE LA BECHE DILLWYN   ELIZABETH   SARAH LLEWELYN
1890 (Harry)   AMY DILLWYN   DILLWYN 1852–1893
                                 1845–1935   (Harry)
                                                   (Essie – m. 1stly
                                                   Fulwar Craven;
                                                   2ndly Richard
                                                   Pakenham)
                                                   Had issue

RICE MANSEL NICHOLL 1875–1959
(assumed 1904 surname DILLWYN on his
marriage to Harriet Gilbertson of Pontardawe)

Olga Welbourn   COLIN LEWIS DILLWYN
1908–1998   1912–1940
                           (K.i.a. at Dunkirk)

his grandfather's name to his own when he came of age to become John Dillwyn Llewelyn) was able to follow his pioneering researches into photography, botany and all his other scientific interests, secure in the income from his extensive estates. Lewis, however, had to chance his arm at various business enterprises none of which was particularly successful, and some of which were unprofitable enough to take him to the verge of bankruptcy.

Another and more direct consequence of John Dillwyn Llewelyn's taking possession of his inheritance in January 1831 was that Lewis Weston and Mary Dillwyn had then to move out of their Penllergaer mansion and look for another home for themselves and their remaining children, the two daughters Fanny and Mary and seventeen-year-old Lewis. Happily they soon found the perfect answer in what had once been described as 'an ideal marine villa', an elegant Georgian house called Sketty Hall situated in idyllic parkland and overlooking the sea on the edge of the Vivian estate at Single-ton. Once the property had been seen by his children Lewis Dillwyn had no option but to settle the matter there and then: 'All the family were so crazily in love with the house that I wrote this evening and offered £3,800 for it and the fixtures and Sketty Hall has become mine.'

Shortly before moving into his new home Lewis Dillwyn was elected as one of the two Members of Parliament for Glamorgan in the first Reform Parliament of 1832 and from then on looked to young 'Lewy' to take over some of the routine responsibilities of his Cambrian pottery. Unfortunately in the long term Lewy, like his father and brother, was more devoted to scientific research than to running a factory, and he accepted his role as manager more from family obligation and the need to earn his living than from any personal inclination. For a while the pottery flourished, artistically at least, especially when Lewy married a wife who took a hand in designing some of its wares; but the younger Dillwyn lacked his father's Quaker instinct for enlightened self-interest in his business dealings, and even at this early stage in his long career as an entrepreneur the seeds of future financial insecurity were already being sown.

On the maternal side Amy's background was equally distinguished and even more unconventional. Her mother Elizabeth (always known as Bessie) was the daughter of Sir Henry De la Beche, only son of Colonel Thomas Beach, a Jamaican plantation owner who, believing himself to be descended from a great Norman family, had changed his name to the more aristocratic sounding De la Beche. Even without his grandiloquent surname De la Beche could claim to be a member of one of the oldest families of landed gentry in Wiltshire, the Beaches of Keevil and Steeple Ashton; so Henry De la Beche had every reason to feel proud of his ancestry, spurious or genuine.

Following in his father's footsteps young Henry De la Beche first embarked on a career in the Army but, after being ignominiously expelled from the military college at Great Marlow for an act of hot-headed indiscipline, he beat a strategic retreat into the field of geological research. Travelling the country with a team of surveyors he led a life of considerable laxity and, being a man of extremely unorthodox views, indulged in various liaisons which were sometimes indiscreet – including the fathering of at least one illegitimate child, a daughter called Rosalie Torre. Having lost the income from his Jamaican plantations after the abolition of the slave trade Henry was obliged to make his own way in the world, and determined to achieve the scientific distinction his talents warranted. In 1818 he married Letitia Whyte the daughter of Captain Charles Whyte of Lough Brickland, Co. Down, and their daughter Bessie (Amy's mother) was born at Geneva in December 1819 while De la Beche was carrying out his geological research on the Continent. Not long after Bessie's birth De la Beche separated from his wife amid mutual accusations of infidelity and neglect, and within a few months of their parting Letitia became the mistress of Major-General Henry Wyndham, an illegitimate son of the Earl of Egremont. Wyndham, a veteran of Waterloo and a man of thoroughly dissolute character, kept Letitia De la Beche in this compromising position over many years – thus effectively depriving her both of her family and her position in society.

Having been abandoned by her mother while still a child Bessie De la Beche spent most of her early life travelling around the country with her father on his various geological expeditions. Artistically inclined but without formal education and a settled background, Bessie grew up in a highly unconventional environment often enlivened by the company of her father's natural daughter Rosalie whom she accepted as a sister and who was one of the few women to whom she could turn for comfort and guidance. In 1837 De la Beche arrived in Swansea as superintendent of a national mineralogical survey and, with Bessie as his companion, took up temporary residence at a miniature mansion near the sea front called Lilliput. As soon as he arrived he sought out his old scientific friend Lewis Weston Dillwyn at Sketty Hall. Bluff in manner and a thoroughly congenial man of the world he quickly became a favourite of the whole Dillwyn family and, on finding Lewis Dillwyn unmarried but looking for a bride, lost no time in introducing him to his only eligible daughter.

Very shortly afterwards Bessie De la Beche was a frequent visitor to Sketty Hall, and she and Lewy found they had a great deal in common. On a beautiful day in May 1838 Lewy walked down to Lilliput from Sketty in order to propose to his dearest Bessie and, he said, 'the result of the interview was that this has been the happiest day of my life'. The weather was perfect, there was a fine crimson sunset and a new moon and the Dillwyns and De la Beches were on their way to becoming one united family, much to the delight of the two distinguished fathers.

Ironically the union of the two families brought together two distinctly different social and cultural backgrounds. Lewy's grandfather William Dillwyn, as the close ally of Benezet and Clarkson, had been instrumental in the abolition of the negro slave trade in 1807, whereas Bessie's grandfather Colonel Thomas Beach had been a substantial beneficiary of the slave trade. Indeed the cessation of the trade had materially weakened the position of the De la Beches to the point where Henry had been obliged to make his way as a professional geologist rather than rely on the diminished income from his estates. Only an exceptionally well-informed reader would have appreciated the paradox of the marriage announcement in the papers:

> Friday 17 August 1838 at St Mary's Church Swansea by the Rev. William Hewson, Lewis Llewelyn Dillwyn, younger son of Lewis Weston Dillwyn Esq. to Elizabeth daughter of Henry Thomas De la Beche of Hulse Hall in the Island of Jamaica.

After the marriage ceremony bride and bridegroom drove from Swansea to Sketty Hall to pay their respects to the groom's parents and then on to Penllergaer, where the mansion had been vacated by Lewy's affluent brother John Dillwyn Llewelyn in order to give the honeymoon couple a suitably impressive venue for the start of their married life.

Early Years at Parkwern and Hendrefoilan

After their honeymoon was over Lewis and Bessie Dillwyn returned to Swansea to make their home at Burrows Lodge, a substantial house which overlooked the harbour in an area just beginning to become unfashionable as a result of the increasing development of the docks. Lewis had chosen to reside there firstly because he was not a wealthy man like his brother, and secondly because it afforded him easy access to the Cambrian and Glamorgan potteries in the Strand which provided him with his main source of income. For Bessie it was her first real home after years of unsettled life and she soon began to relish her public role as the wife of a prominent businessman who was pleased to see her take an active part in the work of the pottery. She had never enjoyed the luxury (or suffered the burden) of unlimited leisure and she found genuine fulfilment in helping Lewis create new patterns and designs. Having inherited her father's skill as an artistic draughtsman she was instrumental in producing the Etruscan ware which was a speciality of the Cambrian pottery at this period, and her talented sketches from classical originals still survive to prove her ability as a designer.

In the summer of 1839 Bessie gave birth to her first child after a difficult pregnancy which made her realize more clearly than ever how much she had lost when her parents had separated so many years earlier. Her father may have been a wonderfully entertaining companion but he could not give her the security of a loving mother and, brought up as she was in a man's world, she felt totally bewildered and apprehensive during her confinement. Years later she wrote to her eldest daughter (who was christened Mary De la Beche Dillwyn but was always known as Minnie) urging her to beware of old wives' tales during pregnancy:

> Remember, dearest Minnie, that until your birth I was as strong and active as a woman could be and never had a day's discomfort from illness. Had I had a mother's care in my early married life I should never have lost my health as I did but I was thrown on my own ignorance and erred from want of anyone to interest themselves in me to give me good advice and information.

Concerned about his wife's worrying state of health after Minnie's birth Lewis took her on an extended holiday to the West Country and set about finding a more spacious and salubrious house for his growing family. His father was reluctant to see them go but saw the need to improve Bessie's health, as he noted in his diary: 'My dear Lewis is 28 and he has this day left Burrows Lodge on account of the necessity of his wife's absence for a year and her subsequent residence in some higher situation which makes a sad break up of our happy domestic circle.' By the autumn Lewis was back in Swansea and found exactly what he was looking for as a new home. A large house called Parkwern on the main Sketty road, situated only a short distance from his father's Sketty Hall, had become available for rent and Lewis was able to secure a two-year lease on the property.

Within a few months of their moving into Parkwern the young Dillwyns were overjoyed to announce the birth in April 1843 of a son and heir christened Henry De la Beche, and old Lewis Weston was pleased to note in his quaint phrase that 'all in the straw are going on well'. Behind the scenes, however, all was not as blissful as it seemed because, just as Harry was born, the 'happy domestic circle' was threatened by a breath of scandal that raised a ghost from the past which the family had hoped was safely hidden away.

Ever since being divorced by Henry De la Beche, Bessie's mother Letitia had lived with General Wyndham as his acknowledged mistress, travelling with him throughout Europe and maintained by him in a fine house in Mount Street, Mayfair. However, after sixteen years in this invidious position Letitia tired of Wyndham's infidelity and quarrelled bitterly with the man who had ruined her reputation in society. Wyndham retaliated cruelly by calling her a thief and a liar and had her ejected from their Mayfair establishment amid a flurry of savage recrimination, including a further charge by General Wyndham that she was constantly intoxicated. Letitia, heart-broken by such callous behaviour, left London to join her widowed mother in her native Ireland. It would have been bad enough if awareness of the scandal had been confined to a few connoisseurs of society tittle-tattle, but worse was to come when in 1843 Letitia's mother chose to publish a blow-by-blow account of the imbroglio in a slim volume entitled *Statement and correspondence upon the Ill Treatment of Lady De la Beche*. Queen Victoria had recently conferred a knighthood upon Henry De la Beche for his services to geology and Letitia was quick to take advantage of her estranged husband's new title to gain extra publicity for her wrongs, pointing out that 'the treatment which Lady De la Beche received at the hands of her husband was such as to render it impossible for her to live with him'.

Within a few months of the publication of this extraordinary exposure of marital unhappiness poor Letitia De la Beche had died in obscurity in Dublin but the effect of her revelations upon the Dillwyns was traumatic. The man and wife whose misconduct was so mercilessly chronicled were Bessie's parents, her adored father and lost mother; their most private affairs exposed to the world after having been discreetly hidden for more than a decade. At a time when Bessie was trying to put her unorthodox upbringing behind her, and Lewis was consolidating his status as a man of business with parliamentary ambitions, such a grotesque revelation could have strained their own marriage to breaking-point. But they were made of sterner stuff than false pride and pretension and nothing remotely suggests they either lost confidence in each other or forfeited the support of their immediate family. In order to overcome the crisis they closed ranks, ignored the gossips and trusted in each other.

It was against this stormy but essentially reassuring background that on a May morning in 1845 Lewis Weston Dillwyn, still hale and hearty at 65, walked to Parkwern from Sketty Hall 'without any suspicion of the event' to find that at half-past twelve a new grand-daughter, another 'chick' as he called her, had been born there – a girl who was to be named Elizabeth Amy Dillwyn.

Once the reverberations of the Lady De la Beche affair had faded away life at Parkwern settled down into a genial normality. Right from the start of his married life Lewis Llewelyn Dillwyn created a civilized and cultivated atmosphere in which his son and daughters were taught by example and precept the responsibilities of their fortunate position in society. Though far from being bohemian or undisciplined, their style of life was unconventional and unfettered by many of the taboos now regarded as typically Victorian. The presence in the young family of De la Beche's natural daughter Rosalie, affectionately known as Rosie by all the children, was an effective bar to strait-laced ideas of morality. Lewis would talk to Minnie, Harry, and Amy as sensible and intelligent human beings with views of their own, never treating them as juveniles to be seen and not heard. The embodiment of many of the Quaker attributes of his father and grandfather, he adopted a forthright approach to his children that left a permanent impression on them all and on Amy in particular, who showed a lifelong aversion to hypocrisy and humbug of every description.

As the youngest of three, Amy was naturally a favourite with her two elderly grandfathers and even as a child derived a great deal of stimulation from the company of these highly gifted men who were also wonderfully good companions, full of gusto and sheer fun. As she sat at the knee of grandfather Dillwyn she would have heard exciting tales of the Rebecca Riots which had occurred just two years before she was born and in which her father and her Uncle John of Penllergaer had taken an active and dangerous role. The farmers and peasants of west Wales, incensed by the intolerable burden of toll-gate charges, had rampaged through the country districts in women's clothes, demolishing every turnpike gate they could lay their hands on. In their capacity as local magistrates Amy's father and uncle had led a small force of police to the village of Pontarddulais, lain in wait for the marauding Rebeccaites, and then engaged them in hand-to-hand combat until they were finally routed and arrested. Old Lewis Weston was a dedicated supporter of law and order and would have retailed the events at Pontarddulais to Amy with enormous relish and bravura. Only a few years after the Rebecca Riots her grandfather De la Beche had played an equally enthusiastic part in the suppression of the great Chartist demonstration on Kennington Common in 1848 when he had busily handed out cutlasses in the stables of the Scotland Yard Police Office to London's special constables, and had been disappointed to find that the great battle he had anticipated turned out to be a cowed and orderly gathering of frustrated revolutionaries. Back at Parkwern, with an audience of enthralled grandchildren, Sir Henry's vivid account of his role in quelling the riot-that-never-was would have lost nothing in the telling.

Both of Amy's grandfathers were major figures in the scientific world of the 1840s and attracted to Swansea some of the leading savants of the period, all of whom helped to furnish for the young Dillwyn family a cultural environment that could hardly have been bettered anywhere in the country. At the end of 1847 grandfather Dillwyn was working hard to organize the detailed preparations for the British Association Meeting in Swansea, but on hearing some disturbing news about his beloved little Amy, he spent some of his valuable time checking that all was well at Parkwern.

> This morning we heard from poor Lewis that our precious little Amy's arm had been cauterised last evening for the supposed bite of a mad dog but on going about to enquire I was rejoiced to satisfy myself not only that there was no appearance of madness but that the spaniel, tho' a stranger, was not and could not have been mad. In short it seems to be admitted that no mad dog goes a'courting.

As long as she remained the baby of the family Amy enjoyed the favoured position occupied by her since birth but, unhappily for her, the Dillwyn

14

household was not yet complete because when she was seven years old her mother gave birth to another daughter Sarah, always known as Essie. From that time on Amy's little nose was firmly knocked out of joint. Being neither the youngest nor the first born nor a boy she no longer had any privileges in the family hierarchy and as time went on she began to realize that her mother's (and to a lesser degree her father's) interest was centred on Essie rather on her. Her innate independence was thus further strengthened by the awareness of having to stand on her own feet come what may.

Essie's arrival also caused her father to look again at the need for buying a house of his own instead of leasing accommodation – something that would be suitable for a growing family and for a man of some substance in Swansea society. Lewis Weston once more came to the rescue by offering his younger son a large plot of land at Hendrefoilan in the gentle hills above his own Sketty Hall. By the early 1850s Lewis had sold off his financial interest in the potteries in order to provide himself with some ready money with which to buy a home; and so he was delighted to accept his father's offer of the Hendrefoilan site and begin building a fine mansion (at a cost of some £14,000) that would finally do justice to his social status. Solidly constructed in the neo-Gothic style the house was to incorporate a magnificent stained-glass window on the principal landing and the carved initials of Lewis and Bessie on the north wall. Although personally unpretentious, and even democratic in his political views, Lewis was proud to include in the stained glass the heraldic coats of arms of both the Dillwyns and the De la Beches in such a way as to suggest that both families could point to an established ancestral line rather than appear to have emerged from nowhere like so many of the *nouveaux riches* in the mid-nineteenth century.

When Hendrefoilan House was nearing completion Lewis Dillwyn seized an opportunity that was to set the pattern for the rest of his life and substantially influence the lives of his children. His father had sat in the Reform Parliament for five years as one of the country members, and by now he himself had developed markedly radical political ideas which he wanted to put into practice. In 1855 on the death of John Henry Vivian, the great industrialist who had represented Swansea for over twenty years, Lewis put his name forward as Liberal candidate in the by-election. He made no secret of his unorthodox views on matters of church and state and, reminding his audiences of his liberal forebears and his consistent advocacy of religious freedom, he was swept into the House of Commons by the almost unanimous support of Swansea's largely Nonconformist electorate. Thus began a career that was to continue for the next forty years and to establish Hendrefoilan as one of the political powerhouses in south Wales.

Unfortunately the elation of this parliamentary success was soon tempered by the deaths of both Lewis Weston Dillwyn and Sir Henry De la Beche, the one in April and the other in the following August. Nevertheless Lewis was left with the consoling thought that both had lived long enough to see him and their grandchildren firmly settled into a permanent home at Hendrefoilan and into the mainstream of Swansea's public life. By the time she was ten Amy's future seemed to be assured, with few clouds on the horizon and everything to hope for. She moved into the brand new mansion with a retinue of household staff made up of butler, cook, maids and garden-ers, as well as a series of governesses and tutors whose job it was to teach the children all they needed to know to take their proper place in the world. Their father, Lewis Llewelyn Dillwyn, MP, left them in no doubt that they belonged to a family of considerable distinction and antiquity both in social and, just as important, in intellectual terms. Much was expected of them because they had a long and (generally) honourable tradition of public serv-ice behind them which made Hendrefoilan the outward and visible sign of rank based not on snobbery but on social responsibility.

This is not to say that Amy's formative years were solemn or dull. With her parents frequently away in London on parliamentary business and with her elder sister Minnie virtually in charge of the household, Amy quickly learnt to accept the rough-and-tumble of domestic life and play her part in bringing up young Essie. But her real favourite was her brother Harry, just two years her senior but like most boys far less mature than his sisters. He shared with her in all sorts of exciting games, romping through the extensive woodland around the house, organizing moth-hunting expeditions by candle-light, and invariably giving Amy the excuse to get blissfully wet and muddy and generally act the tomboy role which came so naturally to her. Harry for his part, having no brothers, treated her as though she were just another boy as eager as he was for every ounce of fun possible. From her infancy Amy was accustomed to climbing trees, wearing rough-and-ready clothes and boots, swimming at any opportunity, and fishing from small boats in Swansea Bay. Her attitude then and later was always the same: 'Take me as you find me; if there's no harm in it then there is nothing wrong with it and I am not ashamed of being myself.'

When she was about eleven her parents realized that her somewhat quiz-zical look was not simply the result of her having an enquiring mind, but had a much more basic cause: she was terribly short-sighted. Her father took her to a London oculist and from that time on she had to wear glasses, which did nothing to enhance her rather plain and intellectual appearance and became a minor but irritating social burden to her as she grew older and had to think about finding herself an eligible suitor. Not to be an heiress was one thing but not to be beautiful as well was another. Whereas Minnie and Harry had inherited their father's handsome appearance. Amy was more like her mother who for all her artistic talents could never have been called a beauty. What Amy had inherited was an unusual degree of intelligence which combined with a determined personality to make her a difficult child for her many private tutors to handle. Years afterwards Amy invited one of her former governesses, Susannah Beer, to lunch at her London home and after Miss Beer had gone recollected with total candour what an awkward pupil she must have been. 'It seemed so strange to see her again. She was the only governess I ever had who didn't hate me, I think, and could anyhow get on with me. I wonder *why* she got on with me? I suppose she let me have my own way pretty much, for else we should surely have had rows together.'

It was obvious that genteel lady teachers were no substitute for her two exuberant grandfathers and that Amy sadly missed the fun and the intellectual stimulation which they had brought into her early life. Her close family circle was further depleted with the death in the autumn of 1858 of Bessie's half-sister Rosie who had lived with the Dillwyns as a kind of honorary aunt for many years. Harry was away at boarding school when Minnie wrote to tell him that Rosie had died of a heart attack and was to be buried with her father Sir Henry De la Beche at Kensal Green. Harry's response was remarkably sensitive for a boy of fifteen and also extremely revealing about his slightly deferential attitude towards his younger sister. 'Like you I cannot understand that I shall never see her again here, though I feel very miserable and lonely indeed. I don't think I shall be able to realise it till I come home and see you all. Poor Amy, she must have felt it very much for she is cleverer than us two and feels it more suddenly and understands it sooner.' Even in her early teens Amy was already showing that special kind of awareness that set her apart from many girls of her age and social class and even from her own closest friends and relations.

But like any other family the Dillwyns had their good times as well as their bad and Amy never missed an opportunity of enjoying the ordinary pleasures of life. One of her first excursions into the social life of Swansea was on the occasion of her Aunt Mary's unexpected marriage in 1857. Mary Dillwyn, a maiden lady in her early forties, had been her mother's companion at Sketty Hall for many years, occupying herself in good works and in helping her talented brother John Dillwyn Llewelyn with his pioneering experiments in photography. Not long after the local copper magnate, Henry Hussey Vivian, had founded St Paul's Church at Sketty the new vicar, the Reverend Montague Welby, proposed to Mary Dillwyn and was duly accepted. Welby, a tall, handsome and distinguished man, belonged to an old Leicestershire family and was related to the first Baron Welby of Denton Manor; so Aunt Mary was thought to have done very well for herself by surprising all the gossips who had written her off as an old maid.

Less unexpectedly, but no less happily, Minnie Dillwyn soon followed her aunt up the aisle of Sketty Church when she married John Cole Nicholl of Merthyr Mawr. The Nicholls of Merthyr Mawr were one of the most influential families in Glamorgan. John's father had been Member of Parliament for the Glamorgan Boroughs and his grandfather, Sir John Nicholl, a prominent Tory lawyer and judge. His mother was Jane Harriot Talbot, the formidable sister of the very wealthy landowner and railway magnate Christopher Talbot, MP, of Margam and Penrice, whose younger sister Emma had married John Dillwyn Llewelyn of Penllergaer. By marrying Johnny Nicholl, Minnie had brought together even more closely three of the most powerful families in south Wales and her wedding was celebrated in great style.

On a rainy day in May 1860 Minnie's uncle the Reverend Montague Welby proudly officiated at her marriage ceremony in St Paul's Church, Sketty, which attracted all the most prominent people in Glamorgan as well as a large contingent of the Volunteer Corps in full-dress uniform and a military band playing spirited marches in the downpour. Not in the least subdued by the elaborate ritual of a society wedding Amy Dillwyn was chief bridesmaid to the sister she called 'my dearest old Wyn' and just for once the tomboy was prepared to look her best in white tarlatan and a white tulle bonnet trimmed with rose-coloured hearts-ease, processing with little Essie and doing her utmost to look grown up and responsible. As the men of the Volunteer Corps marched through Sketty village up to Hendrefoilan to be reviewed by Christopher Talbot, the bride and groom drove to Sketty Hall to pay their respects to old Mrs Lewis Weston Dillwyn who was too infirm to attend the church, and then went on to Penrice Castle in the heart of Gower (which the Talbots had lent to them) for the first stage of a honeymoon planned to take them on a six months' tour of Europe.

Not long afterwards John Cole Nicholl, a mature man of 37 who had been educated at Eton and Christ Church and served his country as a

Brigade Officer in South Africa and the Mediterranean, received a precocious note from his fifteen-year-old sister-in-law Amy telling him of the marriage festivities at Hendrefoilan House and anticipating similar pleasures at Margam Castle. 'I heard yesterday that Mr and Mrs Hussey Vivian are going to Margam Castle for the 7th June. I hope there won't be too many people else I shall feel I had no business there because you see I'm not out yet. It is an immense comfort to me that although I have lost Minnie she isn't wasted upon you. Please give my love to Minnie and as much of it as you choose to take for yourself from Your affectionate sister (hang the 'in law') Amy Dillwyn.'

This was the high-spirited girl, not yet 'out', for whom at her presentation at Queen Victoria's court two years later 'high and mighty Majesty' held no fears.

Debut into Society

On Saturday 28 February 1863 Amy Dillwyn made her debut into Society. She and her proud parents had travelled from Swansea to London a week in advance of the great day, and at noon on the Saturday set off in the family carriage from her home at 10 Prince's Terrace, Knightsbridge, for the short but momentous journey to St James's Palace. She found that Piccadilly was jammed solid with the carriages of all the other debutantes and sat impatiently in Albermarle Street for almost an hour 'stared at ad lib by a lot of ladies' maids and housekeepers and one or two gentlemen who amused themselves with walking up and down looking at us. All the ladies' maids seemed much struck with my hair. It had been beautifully done by Roland and many of them stopped opposite our carriage to look at my head from various points of view as I moved'. Eventually she found her way into the main ante-room of the reception area of the Palace and was faced with a scene of such fairy-tale splendour that even she was tempted to become almost (but not quite) lyrical in her description:

> I think I never saw anything half as pretty as that room was. There was a sea of ladies in magnificent dresses and jewelry all sitting down and a kind of surf of gentlemen in various handsome uniforms standing all round against the wall . . . You know it's no use expecting me to describe dresses because I never could and never can. As for the jewelry it's hopeless to think of telling you about that. If you want to get a notion of what I saw in that line you had better think steadily about nothing but diamonds, emeralds, rubies, opals, pearls and turquoises for the next hour . . . One lady wore splendid amethysts and diamonds all over her head and dress in every possible and impossible place. Altogether it was the prettiest scene I ever saw.

That she saw so much was more of a tribute to her acute intelligence than her eyesight, because she was not wearing her glasses which she felt would have detracted from the dignity of the occasion until she noticed that another woman from Wales, the famous bluestocking Lady Charlotte Schreiber, 'wore her spectacles all through everything at the drawing-room which struck me as being rather an idea for there were heaps of short-sighted people there'. The day after letting Minnie have all her news of the presentation there was yet more famous jewellery to be seen, this time at Garrards where they were displaying the Prince of Wales's wedding presents to Princess Alexandra, and again Amy's critical faculty came into its own. 'It is a magnificent diamond and pearl necklace and two handsome brooches of diamonds in the form of the Prince of Wales plume. But I was not much struck by the guard ring – beryl, emeralds, ruby, turquoise and jacinth, nor yet by the lockets for the bridesmaids – pink coral and diamonds.'

Her matter of fact realism softened a little as the royal wedding festivities got under way in earnest, and she was quite happy to take some advantage of her father's influential position as an MP and director of the Great Western Railway in order to join the select group waiting to greet the Princess when she arrived at Paddington Station on 7 March 1863 after her long journey from Denmark. 'The Princess is very short and very pretty and good-tempered looking', commented Amy who could also spare a thought for the wretchedly miserable 'Widow of Windsor' who considered the rejoicing somewhat out of place when her dearest Albert was not there to share it: 'I feel intensely loyal to the Queen tonight because no one has said anything about her all day.' A week later Amy had a more leisurely view of the royal bride when she went for the first time to what was soon to become Princess Alexandra's favourite church, All Saints, Margaret Street, famous for its fine music and its high ceremonial, and afterwards strolled through the Zoological Gardens which was part of the Sunday ritual of fashionable society:

> There we saw the Prince and Princess of Wales with Prince and Princess Christian (Alexandra's parents) and their other children. The Princess of Wales is certainly very pretty and much nicer looking than her sister Princess Dagmar. I wonder if it is true that she is to marry the eldest son of the Emperor of Russia? Thackeray was also in the Gardens and we also saw Professor Huxley.

Two months later Amy accompanied her future fiancé Llewellyn Thomas to a concert at Covent Garden, carefully chaperoned by his mother and sister, and once more found herself in the presence of the royal newly-weds. 'The Princess was one of the prettiest women in the house which isn't saying much as there were very few nice-looking ones there.' In the same week she exercised her privilege as a recent debutante and celebrated her birthday by going with her parents to a drawing room held by the Princess

21

of Wales at Marlborough House, greatly enjoying the relaxed atmosphere that always surrounded the Prince of Wales's wordly entourage. 'A tremendous squash and a particularly pretty sight it was. I thought it very amusing. We left Prince's Gardens to go to it at 12 and did not get back till nearly 6½. The royal party there consisted of the Prince and Princess of Wales, Princess Louise of Hesse and the Duke and Duchess of Cambridge.' Observant as ever Amy noticed that Alexandra was already beginning to show the telltale signs of the physical strain that was soon to partially cripple her as a result of the hectic social life imposed on her by her husband's compulsive socializing and chronic infidelity. 'Poor thing, she looked tired enough when I passed her today.' She might even have guessed that the Princess was already expecting her first child, the hapless Eddy, Duke of Clarence, who was born in the following January.

Whatever her private thoughts on royal weddings Amy at this time was much more concerned about her own relationship with Llewellyn Thomas of Llwynmadoc. From the days when they had played together as children Amy and Llewellyn had been regarded by their respective families as ideally matched, and now that she had reached the age of eighteen and been successfully launched into society the time seemed ripe for them to come together. She was the obviously gifted and unusually intelligent daughter of Swansea's Member of Parliament and her suitor was the sole heir of a wealthy mid-Wales landowner and colliery magnate named Henry Thomas who was chairman of the county magistrates. Llewellyn had been an old school chum of her brother Harry and their fathers had worked harmoniously together as pillars of the Glamorganshire and Brecon legal establishment. Financially speaking, as a younger sister in a family of four, Amy did not have a substantial fortune to offer in the way of a marriage settlement, but Llewellyn's father was quite capable of making up any monetary deficiencies and his only son stood to inherit one of the richest properties in south Wales. On the other hand, an alliance with the Dillwyns would have given the Thomases, who were not yet firmly established among the country élite, an entrée to wider social and political circles. Money alone could not open every door but a combination of Llewellyn's potential wealth and Amy's social position was full of promise for their joint future.

Not that Amy was easy to win. A born tomboy, only reluctantly reconciled to accepting the decorous attitudes of a young lady in mid-Victorian society, her passionately independent personality needed to be carefully treated, and her sharp intellect tended to deter quite a number of the not very bright young men she met socially. Her dry wit and keen sense of the ridiculous made her a fairly formidable companion even at the age of eighteen and like her elder sister she wanted a husband who could also be a true partner not merely an adoring lover. After a few years of married life with Johnny Nicholl of Merthyr Mawr, Minnie had found her high hopes had not been fulfilled in the way she would have wished. 'I cannot find a companion in him,' she wrote in her diary, 'only a loving and adoring friend. A more indulgent husband no one need desire yet if I could share his pleasure and his business I should require less of his indulgence. When I married I thought to be his second self but I am my own self; perhaps better so.' With Minnie's example before her and conscious of how alike she and her sister were in their strong-willed independence, Amy experienced a young girl's natural doubts and apprehensions about embarking on a lifelong commitment to marriage. She was nevertheless keenly, almost painfully, aware of her social obligations and of the duty she was expected to perform. Llewellyn was perplexed by her nervousness to the point where he gently charged her with a certain coldness towards him. Reading over his passionate letters long afterwards she recalled how mistaken he had been. 'Oh, if he had but known the struggles of my mind at that time. Why, I was like a furnace with an unceasingly fanned and increasing flame . . .'

One quiet Sunday morning in October 1863 Llewellyn came to Amy as she sat alone in the morning-room at Hendrefoilan which looked out across the terrace to the sea and asked her to marry him. She accepted his proposal as the natural culmination of a friendship that had linked them since their childhood. In the evening her mother and Minnie came to her room, and the three women sat together till the small hours animatedly discussing the arrangements to be made and setting Amy's mind at ease about the responsibilities of marriage. The next morning Llewellyn left for his home at Llwynmadoc to carry the good news to his mother and his only sister Clara who immediately travelled down to Neath to meet Amy at the home of Llewellyn's grandmother Mrs Alicia Evan Thomas of the Gnoll. From then on the couple were borne along on a tide of activity with visits to their various relatives, shopping expeditions to London and all the exciting preparations for a society wedding. Llewellyn presented her with a beautiful jewel box, a splendid engagement ring of rubies, and a superb bouquet. Chaperoned by Bessie the young lovers were inseparable whether walking through the woodland around Hendrefoilan or laughing at a comedy in the Haymarket Theatre in London. They called at Margam Castle where Amy received an exquisite diamond ring as a wedding present from Christopher Talbot before going on to Merthyr Mawr to receive the congratulations of all Johnny Nicholl's numerous relatives. Amy thus looked forward to a wedding in the spring.

Everything proceeded according to plan until Christmas when the first ill omen appeared. On 26 December Amy heard that Llewellyn's father had died of a heart attack at Dover on Christmas Eve while travelling to Paris on business. This was a major setback for Amy because apart from the personal loss the death of her future father-in-law meant that all her wedding arrangements had to be postponed for several weeks in observance of the usual period of family mourning. It also meant that her fiancé was obliged to attend to the complicated business interests in which his family was involved. Llewellyn was now not only very wealthy, he was also very busy and had correspondingly less time to spend with her. Making the best of it Amy and her parents wrote to tell everyone the sad news, looking forward to happier times in the New Year of 1864 when the marriage details could again be put in hand. Philosophically (and almost prophetically) Amy said farewell to the year that had ended in disappointment and dismay. 'Goodbye to 1863 with all its cares and sorrows and pleasures and goodbye also to the most miserable Christmas time I ever spent. Where will the end of next year find us all? And how many among us will have passed away by then?'

The new year began with bitter east winds and hard frosts warmed only by the news on 10 January that the Princess of Wales had given birth to her first son, Prince Albert Victor. The previous day a slight thaw had set in and Llewellyn took the train to Torquay for a brief winter break before getting on with the onerous work of settling his father's affairs. In his absence Amy amused herself by devoting her time to her newly discovered sport of ice skating with her cousins on the lake at Penllergaer – a sport which she found enthralling even without Llewellyn to escort her as he had for the previous fortnight of perfect skating weather. She had gone to her uncle John at Penllergaer having left Hendrefoilan with the thought that she would be a different woman when the time came to return as Mrs Llewellyn Thomas. But first she had to visit her grandmother at Sketty Hall and accompany Bessie to the little village of Killay to say goodbye to her Sunday School class with a feast of tea and cakes which the children greatly appreciated. When she sat in her bedroom for the last time in her old role as spinster schoolmarm she felt a strong sense of regret mixed with anticipation. 'Oh my darling old room where I sit now. I wonder if I shall ever again write my diary in you? Oh my home, my home, I never thought I loved you so well as now that I am leaving you perhaps never to return as Amy Dillwyn.'

Over at Penllergaer with her cousins Lucy and Elinor Llewelyn she found the weather bright and frosty and it seemed a good idea to go out into the grounds and make up a bonfire. Still an optimist she believed that every-thing would work out satisfactorily despite the setbacks and the delays. But then the blow fell. On 24 February 1864 she learnt from Minnie that some-thing terrible and totally unexpected had happened. 'Today I heard that Llewellyn died at Paris on Monday night. When he went to Torquay I little thought never to see him again. This day four months ago I promised to marry him and now my strange dream is over and I awake to my former existence but my dream will last in my memory for all my life . . . I hear that they are going to lay Llewellyn by his father at Abergwessin. Tomorrow is his birthday on which he would have been 25.' On the day before the funeral she went into the gardens at Hendrefoilan to gather a few snowdrops to send to her father so that he could put them on the coffin for her as a tribute to her lost lover.

Lewis Dillwyn had been in London for the parliamentary session when news of the tragedy had reached him in a telegram from Llewellyn's mother in Paris. He learnt a little later that the cause of death was smallpox, and it became his melancholy duty to arrange for the carriage of the young man's body from France to south Wales and then to attend the funeral at the little cemetery at Abergwessin where the Thomas family were lords of the manor. He wrote in his diary that evening: 'The procession left Llwynmadoc at 10 a.m. and was attended by a large concourse of tenants and freeholders. I never attended a funeral so large in which there seemed to be such general and real sorrow.'

But few of the many mourners could have felt as Amy did. She had committed herself to marrying a man who had truly loved her and, having prepared herself to sever all her links with the past, she now found herself back where she had started. From being within reach of a social and finan-cial position that would have made her a woman of considerable consequence in the world she was once again Miss Dillwyn, the unmarried daughter of a father living (if the truth had been told) well beyond his relatively modest means. She was aware that the chance of another suitable match was unlikely in an intensely competitive marriage market where one lost opportunity could quite easily entail a lifetime of quiet spinsterhood and good works, of being simply 'Aunt Amy' to Minnie's sons and daughters.

Her private diary at this crucial turning-point in her life betrays very little explicit emotion but the terseness of the entries shows the strain and tension beneath the laconic record. Like all conscientious Victorian diarists she kept a punctilious note of the state of the weather, carefully recording every change as a preface to her comments on the day's events. Yet writing in the weeks immediately following the news of Llewellyn's death she becomes uninformative about her surroundings. Her brief confused comments 'I don't know', 'Fine day I believe', or 'No rain I think', reflect her stunned detachment from her usual interests and even from reality as she retreated into herself. For a while the old Amy, bold and full of what she called 'the animal enjoyment of life', was submerged into a dull nothingness. One of her favourite comments when temporarily depressed was never more appropriate than it was now: 'Le jeu ne vaut pas la chandelle' – the game was not worth the candle.

Picking up the Threads

After a few weeks of virtual seclusion at Penllergaer with the Llewelyns, who were invariably kind and supportive in every crisis, and at Merthyr Mawr with Minnie and Johnny, Amy was persuaded by her parents to spend Easter in London. Her deep sense of personal loss and her natural religious inclination inevitably induced her to seek solace in the Church. She turned to Christ the Redeemer for spiritual comfort and spent much of her time both worshipping and confiding in her Saviour. But her parents were concerned to see that she did not become a complete recluse as a result of her desire to shun the normal pleasures of the world. With some tact they arranged for her to have Italian lessons, and under the guidance of her tutor Signor Pepoli she discovered the delights of reading Dante and Tasso in the original. Emboldened to try another diversion her mother persuaded her to have music lessons with Madam Sainton Dolby, one of the best teachers in London, who soon convinced Amy that her pleasing contralto voice might well improve with dedicated practice.

Gradually, under these benign influences, she began to emerge from her shell of seclusion and to enjoy once more the world she had given up for lost. While Lewis and Bessie Dillwyn played their full part in London society with an arduous programme of drums, conversaziones and musical evenings, not to mention meeting the great Liberal hero Garibaldi on his triumphant arrival in England, Amy was content with an occasional visit to the theatre and select dinner parties with family friends like Sir Charles Young, the Garter King-of-Arms, who was her next-door neighbour in Knightsbridge. Her first real excursion into the outside world was when Minnie, buoyant and adventurous as ever, cajoled her into setting off on a continental tour designed to make her forget her isolation in a whirl of activity and travel. Johnny and Minnie Nicholl, who had always been fond of foreign tours and were anxious to encourage Amy's renewed interest in life, left their children with their nurses and carried her off to Rotterdam determined to restore her high spirits. As soon as she got on board the steamer *Cologne* Amy's old vivacity reappeared and with it some of her sense of mischief and humour. Sharing a cabin with Minnie and two stewardesses she awoke early in the morning to find her fellow travellers all still asleep and 'snoring a trio'. From Rotterdam and its quaint little dog carts – 'the poor doggies go along so good and quiet' – they took the train to Schevening to hear the Sunday afternoon band concert: 'The bands here go on the same principle as the English ones; viz, rest as long and play as little as possible.' From there the next stop was Amsterdam, 'a very curious old town; nothing but canals and they smell very nasty', but she was awed by the sight of Rembrandt's great picture *The Night Watch* hanging in his native city. Once they crossed the frontier into Germany Amy found the journey far more interesting because she could speak German and dispense with the services of an interpreter. She had been taught the language at an early age by one of her governesses, Miss Pachwald, whom she had described as an absolute tartar. 'Do you know Minnie dear that though you mayn't believe it that woman bullies me until the five hours of my life that I spend with her each morning aren't worth having! I declare Min that she is in a bad temper four days in six at least and without counting Sunday!' But now she actually had an opportunity of speaking the language she had so strenuously learnt she made the most of it. While visiting show places like the ancient university town of Heidelberg she was fascinated by the sight of shops open all day on Sunday and by the beauty of the fireflies, a phenomenon which she had never seen before. After an exhausting tour of the Rhine they travelled back through Cologne to Brussels where they were shown over the battlefield of Waterloo by a veteran who had served under Wellington in 1815. Listening to the old soldier's reminiscences Amy was enthralled by the historic link which made the events of nearly half a century earlier seem like yesterday. Almost a month after leaving England they sailed back to Dover tired but exhilarated, and with Amy successfully shaken out of her doleful lethargy.

Being a woman, and an upper-class woman at that, she was subject to all the limitations that severely narrowed her field of action. Vigorous commitment was what she now needed and wanted, some kind of exceptional activity that would give her life a meaning it had hitherto lacked. For the moment, however, Amy had to be content with the skirmishes of polite society and the gossip of the day. In the long hot summer of 1864 the main talking point was that Lady Florence Paget, who was engaged to be married to the wealthy Mr Chaplin, had bolted with and married the disreputable Marquis of Hastings despite her fiancé's having paid all her debts to the tune of £12,000. It was said of the 'wicked Marquis' that he breakfasted on mackerel fried in gin, caviare on toast, and a bottle of claret. London was outraged and amused and Amy shared in the general amusement. That Amy could interest herself in such social trivia was a clear sign of her return to normality, but as the end of the Season drew near her parents prepared her for the ordeal of returning to their country home at Hendrefoilan with all its memories of her high hopes when she had left it just six months before.

First there was a final flurry of pleasurable engagements. There was the Eton and Harrow cricket match at Lord's with its champagne, salmon mayonnaise, and strawberry ices; then the House of Lords versus the Commons rifle tournament at Wimbledon in which her father was one of the Commons Eleven, followed by a glittering performance of *The Barber of Seville* at Covent Garden with the great stars, Mario and Patti. Sitting in a box with her family and close friends Amy spent the evening in a seventh heaven of delight. She loved opera more than any other form of entertainment and so for an evening at least she could forget the reality that had recently overwhelmed her. When the time came to pack up and leave London Essie was in a perfect fever of excitement to return home, but her sister had not so easily forgotten the last night she spent there and was reluctant to abandon the innocent recreations that had helped to soften the blow.

Her homecoming was made easier by the welcoming presence of Harry down from Cambridge for the long vacation, and all her old love for him returned to revive her flagging spirits. They had always been very close and Harry had suffered a severe accident a few years earlier which made her even fonder of the 'dear old boy' because it made him more vulnerable and less successful than he might otherwise have been. While he was still at boarding school in Bedfordshire his left eye had been seriously injured in some juvenile rough-and-tumble and his father had been compelled to authorize a surgeon to remove it to save him from the risk of total blindness. Though only sixteen at the time Amy had been deeply hurt by her brother's misfortune, as she was quick to see that the disability would make his studies and future career that much more difficult. When she arrived at Hendrefoilan the first thing that she did was go off with Harry and find a quiet spot where they could sit and chat exactly as they had when they were children: 'He and I have been walking about the place and sitting talking in the summer house, and finally I went with him when he went to smoke a pipe in the laundry and we did a deal more conversation while he smoked. And now I am here again in my dear old room having been away nearly six months and feeling as many years older than when I went away.'

Before long she was immersed in a round of social engagements which, if not intellectually very demanding, did help to keep her occupied and amused. She particularly liked visiting Margam Castle, playing croquet on the lawns and applauding Harry as he competed with Christopher Talbot's son and heir Theo in shooting matches on the sands. Unconcerned about preserving the conventional Victorian lady's parasol-protected complexion she spent all her time in the open air and she paid the penalty. 'The scorching sun has pretty well made red Indians of us. Poor dear me! What a state of roast my cheeks are in!'

Back in Swansea she found herself reluctantly caught up in routine chores related to the obligatory, and to her tedious, business of fund-raising such as the Killay Church bazaar where she and her mother were prominent stall-holders. So in the perfect summer weather she went into Swansea with Mama and other members of the family to supervise their stalls at an event designed to part Swansea's more affluent citizens from their money. Despite Amy's moral doubts she was pleased to sacrifice herself in a good cause:

> At our stall we took altogether £62 and I really felt quite ashamed of myself to go taking people's money for things that could be of no use to them. As for getting up raffles, that's really dreadful; between chaffing some people and wheedling others to make them take shares and telling rigmaroles about every article on the stall. Henry Crichton [her cousin Emma Llewelyn's husband] had a quantity of water from the Dead Sea and it was quite astonishing how many bottles of it we sold at 2/6d and 3/6d a bottle.

She felt similar reservations about helping with a tea party for her Killay schoolchildren, much as she wanted her young charges to enjoy themselves: 'I think there is no occasion on which one looks such a fool as at a school-feast being an amateur female footman keeping the cake and tea supplies going. Everyone goes bustling about with an important look and a sort of condescending I'm-not-used-to-this-sort-of-thing-simper.' Even at home there was precious little to do except while away her time with some gentle exercise playing the fashionable game of the moment. 'I can't say I've read anything today; my chief intellectual exertion has been remembering which hoops everyone was going through next at croquet!'

A few days later she was able to raise her intellectual sights a little by riding over to Penllergaer on her newly acquired pony Rantoon which her father had bought her as a special welcome-home present. When she arrived she found the Llewelyns engaged in the kind of scientific pursuits which they had inherited from their Dillwyn grandfather. Her uncle, John Dillwyn Llewelyn, besides being an outstandingly good photographer who had collaborated with Fox Talbot in the earliest days of the camera, was also an eminent natural scientist and astronomer. In order to pursue his study of astronomy more closely he had built an equatorial observatory in the grounds of Penllergaer House, for which his eldest daughter Thereza had laid the foundation stone in 1855. Thereza was now married to Nevil Story Maskelyne, another prominent photographer and astronomer, and the whole family at Penllergaer were avid amateur scientists who were only too glad to encourage cousin Amy to share in their experiments. Knowing her need for distraction and mental exercise they invited her to join them for dinner followed by their own kind of intellectual fun and games. In the evening they all trooped out into the grounds first to try and send up a hot-air balloon which unfortunately caught fire and had to be abandoned, and afterwards took turns to study the heavens from the observatory. 'I looked through Uncle John's big telescope,' wrote Amy, 'and saw the moon which looked like Gruyère cheese and also saw Jupiter and three of his moons; the fourth was eclipsed by himself. Harry and I returned to Hendrefoilan by moonlight. He goes to Merthyr Mawr tomorrow and I shall miss him dreadfully.'

Calling at Penllergaer and sampling its many lively interests invariably aroused Amy's longing for a more rewarding way of life, for a richer experience than she normally enjoyed at home. 'Oh how I should like to be clever. To be able to write good poetry and to understand all languages and express my own thoughts (and of course to have thoughts worth expressing). However, wishing's no use and I must be content to stumble along like the generality of my kind.' And stumble along she did. As long as Bessie Dillwyn was in charge of the Hendrefoilan household Amy had no choice but to exist in her mother's shadow often a little impatient with the constant need to socialize but aware that an MP's daughter, as well as his wife, had certain obligations she could not afford to neglect if her father's popularity was not to suffer. While Papa was in Swansea 'buttering up the shopkeepers' (as Amy somewhat tartly described it) it was Mama's job to 'palaver' with their wives and sustain her leading role in local affairs. One of the most important of Bessie's social commitments was the morning call, when she and Amy did the rounds of visiting all their friends and certain acquaintances and left cards on those who were (officially at least) 'not at home'. The custom was to leave not one but usually three visiting cards, one from Bessie herself and two from her husband, one meant for the lady of the house and the other for the master. 'We called on half a dozen people this morning', noted Amy on one occasion, 'but fortunately most of them were out. What a lot of tea and twaddle there was and leaving of pasteboard.'

Anything that smacked of pretension and condescension was anathema to Amy. She did her duty gallantly, keeping her innermost thoughts for her diary, and it was only when she was by herself in the late evening that she allowed herself her 'reveries', especially about what might have been if her life had not suddenly come to a dead end. 'I feel very strange and dreamy,' she said, 'I never speak of last winter to anyone tho' it is seldom out of my mind.' She understood very clearly the difference between the outward politeness of society and the true feelings of those around her, feelings which were never shown, never discussed and seldom even referred to. Late one summer's evening while sitting alone in her room in the Gothic splendour of Margam Castle after leaving the company of a large party of guests, she reflected on the contrast between appearance and reality.

> When the world seems so beautiful and peaceful it seems almost wrong there should be such unrest and bitterness and grief in it as there is. Probably out of the many people in this house tonight there is not one that has not some bitter memory or disquieting knowledge that will come to his or her mind when the lights are out and the person in bed and no one to see what the face may betray – no one to spy out the secrets. Oh! we all play our game in the world but we all come off the stage at night in our own rooms. And we all then must recognise the things that we put aside for the day in society or pursuits and think we have forgotten or at least not feel their full weight. Of course I have my own array of skeletons and out of their cupboards they will come in spite of locking the door. Now for my skeletons – Bon soir la compagnie!

Outwardly at least Amy appeared to enjoy the long summer days when she could spend most of her time in the open air, but as winter approached she looked around despairingly for a new and demanding pastime to while away the long evenings at home. At last she hit on the idea of knitting a pair of stockings for Harry. She had never tried her hand at knitting before, apart from a pair of warm mittens for a poor old lady in Killay, and anticipating difficulty she ironically suggested she might finish them 'in another year or two perhaps'. A week later when she had knitted about half way down the leg she 'had the pleasure of finding the directions from which I am making it were not at all good so I had to undo nearly all my poor stocking – and most trying to my feelings it was'. By early December she had made progress but had grave doubts which were widely shared: 'All the people who have seen the precious stocking I am knitting for Harry have ridiculed its huge size. Harry tried it on and it is immense – beyond all hope of shrinkage. So

I unravelled it and began yet again on one of smaller dimensions. Nil desper-
andum.' By the New Year she had, with the help of a governess in the
tricky operation of rounding the heel, succeeded in finishing both socks but
now found them if anything to be too small. But whatever their faults
Harry's new stockings were good enough for him to wear them to go
shooting with Papa in the deep snow of a bitterly cold January morning 'to
my great pride'. However trivial the occupation, Amy hated being baffled
or defeated by anything that was worth her perseverance.

With Harry at home she could relive her childhood pleasures. The day
after he christened his new stockings she accompanied him on another
shooting expedition in the little valley below the house at Hendrefoilan
where snow drenched them through to such an extent that: 'When I came
in all the bottom of my petticoat was frozen hard and the only three articles
of clothes I had on that were not wet were my stays, my petticoat and my
flannel waistcoat.'

For the time being Amy (whose idea of pure pleasure was 'kicking up a
dust') could forget about behaving in a ladylike manner as when, one rainy
morning, she and Harry tired of languishing in the house and decided to try
something more spectacular. She persuaded Harry to bring out his saloon
pistol, a small calibre revolver, and looked around for a suitable target to fire
at. Finding nothing to hand she calmly took off her hat, threw it up in the
air, and took turns with Harry to see who could hit it more often. In spite
of his disability Harry hit it twice to her once; his honour as a marksman was
satisfied and her high spirits were given free rein.

While her brother remained at home her life at Hendrefoilan was at least
tolerable so that even a sombre family occasion like the death of their Grand-
mama, old Mary Dillwyn of Sketty Hall, was made more acceptable by the
knowledge that she could lighten the awful solemnity by chatting with
Harry. As she confessed to herself she could not really pretend to mourn her
grandmother because 'there is no affinity between 89 and 18'. She dreaded
the time when Harry would have to return to his studies at Cambridge leaving her without her liveliest companion. 'What shall I do *sans* him?' she
asked, knowing how much she depended on his brotherly affection.

Just before he left Amy persuaded him to go with her to the Wind Street
studio of James Andrews, Swansea's leading professional photographer, so
that they could be taken together for the family album. Enterprising and
unorthodox as ever Amy insisted on having something different from the
usual run of woodenly posed studio portraits: 'I am sick of the popular varie-
ties in photos,' she protested, 'of smirk, lounge, stiffness, studiousness,

frown, simper, idiocy, etc. on the various faces and therefore we were done playing cards together which is I think a quite original attitude to be photographed in.' And of course she was right. Very few mid-Victorians would have chosen to be recorded for posterity as a couple of card-players. The obliging Mr Andrews accordingly took several shots of brother and sister nonchalantly seated opposite each other at the card table, with Amy very much in command both of her faithful Harry and the photographer with a look which very clearly says 'No simpering here please: we are real people in a real situation'.

But when the time came for Harry to leave, Amy was left in solitude to reflect on the first anniversary of Llewellyn's death, writing sadly and realistically: 'Today is the anniversary of the day when the man who loved me best in the world died. It seems strange to look back on the past. I have never felt the same since. I wonder if I shall ever be a lone old woman living on past memories?' Despite this melancholy mood the down-to-earth Amy soon reasserted herself and she asked defiantly: 'Why must women always marry? If I am to be a lone old woman so be it!'

The fear of being an old maid (a particularly depressing prospect in the middle of the nineteenth century) was alleviated for Amy by the knowledge that she could in the last resort turn for consolation to her love of God and seek the opportunity of working for Him as a member of one of the many religious orders.

> I believe the Sisterhoods do actual real work towards civilising the masses but they need more ladies to join them, more labourers in the vineyard. It would I think be the highest privilege to be allowed to give up everything one had and give oneself wholly to God's work; to give up all to Him – time, talents, education, health, strength, money, energies, *everything*. I believe Sisterhoods to be the highest life and, believing so, I don't see how I can be justified in living a lower one; I suppose if I were to fall in love with anyone it might alter the case but unless that were to happen it seems to me nothing would alter my duty. And even in the case I put – of my falling in love – it might be the higher and more acceptable act to put aside that earthly love and give myself more entirely to the Divine Love.

So in her own mind whatever happened to her in the future, be it marriage or Sisterhood, she would always have work to do and always be needed for some specific task. However, being human and being a woman, she kept

Amy Dillwyn's birthplace and her childhood home

Lewis Weston Dillwyn, Amy's paternal grandfather,
in a very early daguerreotype photo of 1841

Sir Henry De la Beche with his grandchildren: Minnie, Harry and little Amy at his knee

Amy in her mourning dress in early spring of 1864

Amy in her engagement dress in the autumn of 1863, wearing her ruby ring

Amy's mother Bessie, born Elizabeth De la Beche

Amy with brother Harry at Park-wern in 1853 with Amy already in charge of her older brother; taken by their Aunt Mary (Dillwyn)

Amy in an undated carte de visite (1860s)

Amy and Harry playing cards in James Andrews's Swansea photo studio, June 1866

Amy (right) with her invalid friend Olive Talbot of Margam Castle, taking the waters at Buxton in 1871

Lewis Llewelyn Dillwyn, leader of the Welsh Liberals in the House of Commons

Essie Dillwyn and her future husband Captain Fulwar Craven of the Grenadier Guards playing a game of dice

Amy in 1853 with her father Lewis Llewelyn Dillwyn, elected Liberal MP for Swansea in 1855

Hendrefoilan mansion, the Dillwyn family home from 1855 to 1892

Amy enjoying life on board the liner Atrato in February 1891 just before the catastrophe she suffered the following year

MUNICIPAL ELECTION,
NOVEMBER 1st, 1907.

CASTLE WARD.

ELIZABETH AMY DILLWYN,
The Independent Candidate.

Printed and Published for the Candidate by J. Thomas & Son, 13, Dynevor Place, Swansea.

Amy's election manifesto as Independent candidate in the municipal election of 1907

An Elector's Reasons why you should
Vote for Miss DILLWYN.

BECAUSE—

1. Her reputation as an Economist in dealing with Public Monies is well established.

2. She has independence of thought and action and is not swayed by mere Party cries.

3. She has the necessary time at her disposal.

4. As a Member of the late School Board, and as a Guardian of the Castle Ward, her attendance to the duties she undertook has always been above reproach.

5. She is a worthy member of one of Swansea's oldest and most honoured families.

Ally Sloper cartoon of Amy at Paddington station in 1904, by the Newport artist Bert Thomas, who later achieved fame in World War I

Amy at her final home at West Cross, Swansea, with one of her renowned cigars

Amy with her dog Crack outside her home at West Cross, now the Mumbles Nursing Home

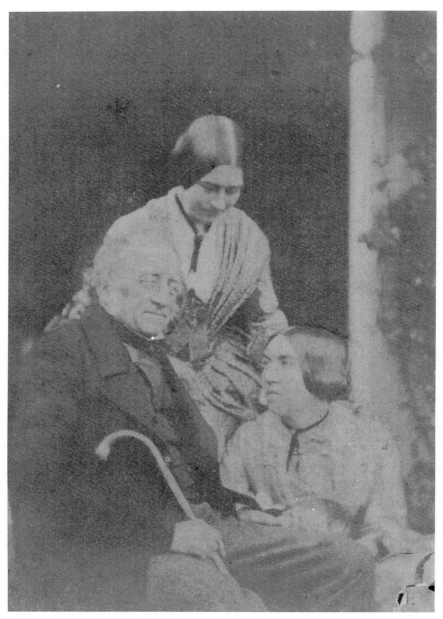

Amy's Mother Bessie with her father Sir Henry De La Beche and her illegitimate half-siser Rosie (centre)

her options open – and the option of romance was not yet ruled out completely.

In this more confident and even defiant mood she was determined to make the best of whatever life had to offer, but her particular vulnerability as a potential spinster came home to her very forcefully when her wealthy friend Henrietta ('Etta') Vivian of Singleton announced her engagement to a Wiltshire gentleman named Major Clement Heneage. Heneage was a professional soldier who had won the VC in the Indian Mutiny, the kind of actively heroic character whom Amy admired intensely and whose bravery she would dearly have liked to emulate if she had had the advantages of a man's career. Philosophically she accepted her friend's good fortune in capturing the gallant Major, but her staunch resolutions were severely put to the test when Etta's pompous brother, Hussey, called at Hendrefoilan to convey the news of the forthcoming marriage.

Henry Hussey Vivian was the eldest of the three sons of John Henry Vivian whom Amy's father had succeeded as Member of Parliament for Swansea. Hussey and his father had built up the Vivian Copper Works in the Hafod district of Swansea into one of the greatest industrial enterprises in the country and Hussey, besides being one of the largest employers of labour in south Wales, was also one of the two Members for the County of Glamorgan. Because his elderly widowed mother stubbornly refused to move out of the Vivian family mansion at Singleton he was obliged to live at Parkwern, the house on Sketty Road where Amy had spent her early childhood. He and his two brothers, Graham and Glynn, had always failed to win favour with Amy and she found Hussey's condescension especially trying when, in talking to her mother, he touched on the delicate subject of spinsterhood. 'Mr H. Vivian walked up here this afternoon and apropos of Etta's engagement delivered a tirade against old maids stating clearly his opinion that a girl who doesn't marry goes contrary to all the laws of the world. "Je vous fais mes compliments" Mr H. V. and beg to differ from your mightiness.' This comment she confided indignantly to her diary, but for the sake of Mama preserved a frosty silence in the face of such crass provocation from the great entrepreneur.

This was only one of many occasions when the insensitivity of the Vivians both irritated and amused Amy Dillwyn. She was highly entertained, for example, by a capital story concerning Glynn Vivian's gauche behaviour during Etta's wedding festivities in December 1865.

The house was full and one of the bridesmaids, Miss Stanley, was asked to sleep in the room that usually belonged to the old nurse they have

had at Singleton for the last fifty years named Sally Lewis. One morning Glynn Vivian felt very ill and wanted some salvolatile so off he
went to the room where he expected to find Sally at 6 o'clock in the
morning. Instead of a grey head a black one lay on the pillow. He
thought it was one of the maids and said. 'Where's Sally?' All the
answer he got was 'Go away, go away!' At last he discovered that he
was speaking to a young lady and stopped to apologise before he went.
At 9 o'clock he was visited by brother Graham in a state of intense
indignation and the whole family I believe scolded him and sat upon
him thoroughly.

In Amy's eyes Glynn Vivian was a conceited vulgarian who thought
himself much more important than he was, a jumped-up scion of the
nouveau riche business class who fancied himself as a first-generation gentleman. Admittedly her own father also belonged to the new business élite but
he had sprung from the Quaker Dillwyns who knew how to behave, unlike
Glynn Vivian who gave himself airs and had more money than sense. About
this time she recorded an encounter with her *bête noire* which epitomized
her intuitive insight into the character of a young man already showing signs
of the dissolute nature that was to cripple him in later life and turn him into
the black sheep of his family, ostracized even by his own brothers: 'In the
morning Papa and I rode into Swansea and then out to see his works. It was
very pleasant riding on such a fine day. We had the felicity of meeting
Glynn Vivian riding in town and really one doesn't often see such a get-up
as his; I never saw a more thorough-looking little snob.'
    Nor was Amy's sense of the ridiculous confined to the menfolk of the
Vivian family. On another occasion after a dinner party with the Hussey.
Vivians at Parkwern she was struck by the engaging eccentricities of her
hostess, Hussey's second wife Caroline, in the presence of several talented
young ladies all of whom had enjoyed the benefit of expensive piano lessons
with private tutors: 'The Hussey Vivians were very kind indeed to us but
Mrs V amused me as much as she always does; she says such very funny
things in the most naive way and without the least idea she is doing anything
odd. Tonight she wanted Mary Bassett to play; Mary refused and hesitated
and shilly shallied, whereupon Mrs V said as if it were the most convincing
argument she could use; "Oh *do* play Miss Bassett – there's no-one here at
all musical." '
    When the time came to forgo the provincial diversions provided by Mrs
Hussey Vivian and to pack her bags ready for another London season she

looked forward with some of her old zest to the enlargement of her horizons – to to the opera, celebrity concerts, the romantic ballrooms, and the whole wide range of metropolitan social life. After a particularly busy day spent riding in Rotten Row and at a festival of music at St Paul's she rounded off the evening with a grand soirée at the Horticultural Gardens: 'The great conservatory was well lit up and looked very pretty; I can't say as much for the people who were there for some of them were very odd looking individuals. I have done so much today that I am quite done up and desperately sleepy.' Only someone who had fully recovered her ability to enjoy life would have done so much and exhausted herself so pleasantly.

So the summer of 1865 passed in a delightful whirl of shopping for new clothes, and walking and riding in the Park where every member of the Upper Ten Thousand delighted to take part in a daily parade of fashion headed by the Prince and Princess of Wales, and where Amy was pleased 'to see and be seen' as she rode in her open carriage with Papa and Mama as escorts. The carriage, newly delivered from Swansea, greatly enhanced the Dillwyn's family ability to hold its own with the best of London society and for the first time Amy could bask in the comfort of her father's social status. When the all too short season came to an end and the time arrived to renew the domestic routines of Hendrefoilan Amy was as reluctant to return home as she had been the previous year but for a very different reason. Having tasted the joys of high society she was extremely sorry to give up, even temporarily, a mode of life she found altogether congenial. Back in her old familiar room overlooking the quiet expanse of Swansea Bay she was almost dismayed, and certainly envious, to receive long letters from her close friend Olive Talbot of Margam and from her sister Minnie who were still amusing themselves in 'Town'. 'It was very trying to me to hear of all the delights of London, of balls, theatres and operas which they are enjoying while I am shut out from them and am vegetating here. How I wish I were there tonight and that I might go to Lady Allen's ball – I *always* enjoy a ball. Oh! I do love balls and dancing and, shall I say, a spice of flirting?'

Instead of dancing the night away in some gilded Mayfair salon with its 'spice of flirtation' she had to make do with assisting the charitable schemes of the newly-appointed vicar of Sketty, the young Mr Edward Brown, whose personality was not at all to her liking and who was destined to become a longstanding cause for complaint, not merely because he read the service far too slowly but also because he constantly pursued her with proposals of marriage she could well have done without. For this highly intelligent twenty-year-old girl Swansea and its worthy causes were rapidly becoming a little mundane after the glamour of the West End and Rotten Row. She was still an impressionable young woman with all the perfectly natural desires of her age and sex. Torn between the conflicting demands of strict religion and innocent pleasure she saw her dilemma very clearly. 'It has struck me tonight what a peculiar mixture I am. Here am I who honestly look forward to being a Sister of Mercy at a Home in some future period of my life and yet taking the liveliest interest in gossip, jewellery, handsome dresses, society and all that sort of thing. I think the real reason is that as long as one does belong to the world of society one must know as much as other people and keep oneself up to their mark. Perhaps it will make it harder finally to give it all up.' She was not to know that soon the dilemma would be resolved for her with no question of her entering a Sisterhood and with long-term consequences she could hardly have foreseen.

Mistress of Hendrefoilan

During the long wet winter of 1866 there were clear signs that Bessie Dillwyn's health was failing. She had never been very robust since the birth of her first child but her courageous spirit and deep loyalty to her family had masked the seriousness of her condition over the previous few years. Bravely carrying out a long series of social functions (which included laying the foundation stone of Swansea's Albert Hall in March 1863) she was reluctant to concede that she could no longer carry out her role as the busy wife of a Member of Parliament who was already one of the most respected Liberal leaders in Wales. By February 1866 Lewis was so alarmed by his wife's condition that he decided to let their town house for the summer, much to the anger and disappointment of his family and especially of Bessie herself, as Amy duly noted, with some sympathy:

> Mama was very vexed and put out at the news and cried violently and worked herself up into a great state of excitement at being told this suddenly and its having been done without her knowledge or consent. Harry is intensely angry that Mama is so upset. The household is in an unpleasant condition tonight and I am also very sorry to think of having at least a year of dreary stagnation down here in Swansea. Oh! I do so *long* to go to London again. Papa and Harry who have their shooting and fishing and who hate society can't understand what pleasure we women find in it. Why! we have nothing else to amuse us and society is not to be had in the country. Besides I *like* London. I like the churches one can go to there and I like even the very pavements that belong to London.

But instead of anticipating the Season and its marvellous opportunities for wearing new dresses, meeting new acquaintances and possibly new admirers, she was compelled to devote more and more of her time to helping the nurse who had been engaged to look after Mama. She had never been particularly close to Bessie but none the less buckled down to the responsibility of caring for her mother even though she suspected her mother had never especially cared for her. 'I'm sure Mama likes Essie so much better than me yet I have tried to give myself up to her in her illness. I can't say I like nursing; in fact I think there are few employments I should dislike so much. However, there's no use growling when I've got to do it.'

Even if Lewis Dillwyn had been rather tactless in brusquely cancelling the family's London season his decision was soon proved correct because within a few months Bessie was dead, and Amy realized with a shock that to all intents and purposes she had become the mistress of her father's establishment at Hendrefoilan. She was not yet twenty-one years old and had no experience whatsoever of the often onerous job of running a large household. Since Minnie was wrapped up in her own steadily increasing family at Merthyr Mawr and Essie was still a child, there was no one to whom Amy could turn for aid and comfort and her immediate reaction was to run away and not return. 'I felt as if there was no one left to help me in all the innumerable small things to be seen to. Miss Buller [the governess] and Steiner [the maid] told me what to do about clothes for myself and Essie for I know nothing about clothes at any time and still less now. And then there were many letters to write and I wrote them all. Dreary, dreary and dismal everything seems. I feel I should like to go right away and not come near the place for the next long time – six months or so, but that cannot be for Papa wishes to stay and I ought to stay with him now.'

Once the immediate impact of her mother's death had faded Amy quickly realized that, however tiresome she might have been in her awkward moments, Mama had also been the mainstay of the whole family. Garrulous and silly by Amy's rigorous standards, Bessie Dillwyn had known exactly how to manage Hendrefoilan with its troublesome servants and their rather unworldly master. Without her guiding hand the comfortable pattern of Amy's life had radically altered. 'I feel rather like a steam engine without a driver puffing about in an objectless sort of way and such an engine usually ends in a runaway or an explosion I think, if left to itself.' In this frame of mind Amy was less than enthusiastic about the day-to-day administrative chores she now had to undertake. She was the first to admit that 'house-keeping is not my forte' and was extremely put out at having to cope with the newly-appointed cook and housekeeper, Madame Nicholas, especially when she learnt that Madame was illiterate and therefore could not be trusted with the domestic accounts. With schoolgirl sarcasm she reported: 'I had the pleasure of discovering that Madame Nicholas can't write at all – a most pleasing quality in a house-keeper, I *don't* think. The kitchen maid *will* be impertinent to her and then Madame Nicholas complains to me. It's very hard that I get bothered by the servants for I'm sure I don't care what they do as long as they leave me alone. I know nothing about anything relating to housekeeping & all I wish is *not* to be bothered.'

But as her experience broadened so did the sense of humour which seldom lay far beneath the cool surface of her personality, and she soon began to take major internal crises in her stride. When her unpopular house-keeper again upset the rest of the domestic staff she refused to join in the general consternation. 'The servants seemed in a row this morning. Madame Nicholas, Fanny Lewis and Harriet all came to me and complained of each other. There really didn't seem to be anything to quarrel about when it was told me, nevertheless quarrelled they had and even got to blows for Madame informed me respecting Harriet – "She pushed me – and I pushed her back, Miss!" with an emphasis and indignation that nearly set me off laughing in her face.' While Amy chafed at being obliged to deal with such minor hostilities she watched with some envy the more exciting activities of rela-tives and friends who did not have to cope with such frustrating trivia.

One day, for instance, she heard a rumour that the egregious Glynn Vivian (ten years her senior but still a bachelor) might marry Lady Theresa Lewis's daughter and her reaction was succinct: 'She must be hard up for a husband poor thing. Perhaps it's not true.' Whether Amy was tasting sour grapes is not clear but she was equally dismissive about another possible suitor, Weston Moggridge, a clergyman cousin who was often the subject of her critical attention because he abysmally failed to measure up to her exacting requirements of a true Christian. Just after his ordination she commented: 'On our return to Hendrefoilan we found the delectable Weston here. It's the first time I have seen him since he has been ordained but I can't say I thought he looked very clerical. He drives me pretty nearly distracted for he's such a boor and so conceited and self-sufficient. Besides I heard him swear this evening. Now that's bad enough for anyone but worse still for a clergyman to do.' When Weston went so far as to get himself engaged to a Miss Giffard, the daughter of his rector, Amy was so peeved that she lapsed into an unashamed outburst of disbelief that was scarcely charitable. 'Well, there's no accounting for taste but I ain't predisposed in favour of Miss Giffard by the only thing I ever heard of her, namely that she accepted Weston. I didn't think the woman existed who would have prom-ised to live with Weston "Till death us do part."'

Still more poignant for Amy was the marriage of plain but affluent Bertha Talbot of Margam to John Fletcher of Saltoun, because the date of their wedding coincided exactly with the anniversary of the day Llewellyn Thomas had proposed to her just three years earlier. Shortly after breakfast at Hendrefoilan the whole Dillwyn family set out for Margam for the great event which, according to Amy's account, 'went off extremely well. A whole heap of the Fletcher clan were staying at the Castle, each one uglier than the other except for Miss Fletcher Campbell who is quite nice looking'. In the middle of the celebrations, among the palatial riches of one of the finest estates in south Wales, Amy could not help comparing her own position with that of Bertha her close friend and almost exact contemporary. 'This day three years ago things looked different to what they do now. All day I have been recalling what happened; how I was asked to marry a man and accepted him, and I wonder if three years from now will find me the inmate of some Sisterhood. Yes, with all my heart I hope and pray for it.'

Other people's weddings and the conventional happiness of other girls of her own age invariably strengthened her inclination to become a member of a religious community far removed from all earthly temptations and satisfactions. Yet she never yielded to such an inclination and for the time being at least she had the excuse that her first duty was to stay at home and look after Essie and her father until Essie eventually 'came out' into society. So instead of sailing to far away places as a Sister of Mercy she sensibly concluded that charity began at home and turned her attention to the conversion of the Nonconformist stronghold of Killay.

Charity begins at Killay

The village of Killay (or Cilâ in Welsh) was at this period a mainly working-class area of poor housing which had attracted a large number of Irish labourers to work on the new railway that was being constructed to link Swansea with the industrial Midlands. The living conditions of the navvies and their families were harsh and often brutal and when Amy first started her charitable visits to the area she found the situation far worse than anything she could have imagined. Anyone more squeamish would have taken one look at such a place and quietly retreated to the solid comfort of Hendrefoilan House just a mile or so along the road, but not Amy. Enlisting the aid of the vicar's wife Mrs Montague Welby, her Aunt Mary, she called at two of the cottages which seemed most in need of help and wrote with calm amazement of the squalor she found there:

> Both were kept by Irish women, wives of two navvies and each had two children less than four years old. I never before saw such thorough sites of untidiness and dirt as those two cottages. Little bits of places they were and yet one of the women told us that in one of these holes lived eight navvies besides herself and husband and two children. Her account of the state of intoxication into which the men get on Sunday was really dreadful. Of course there are some steady exceptions but I am afraid that is the rule. She said her husband went to chapel (Roman Catholic) every Sunday as regularly as could be but she did not accompany him so she is always left there by her husband with eight drunken navvies! Her own expression about her husband's religion was 'He don't care for anyone else so long as he shall be saved.' A queer kind of creed to my mind.

Amy's uncle, the Revd Mr Welby, was keenly aware of the growing influence of both Roman Catholicism and Welsh Nonconformity in Killay and, in an attempt to stem the tide of dissent, had built a new schoolroom in the village to which he hoped to attract a regular class of children for religious instruction while, as Amy said, 'they are young and impressionable so that they may learn they are not mere beasts of the field'. From its inception in 1858 this school had been the special concern of the Dillwyns of Hendrefoilan, and as Amy grew older she had begun to play an active role as teacher and patroness. She found schoolteaching particularly demanding and not always as rewarding as she would have liked, partly because the village had earned an unenviable reputation: 'Oh dear! I think trying to civilize Killay is very hard work, and perhaps (in fact probably) all work to no purpose especially when people begin to talk of having a policeman at Killay because of its being so uproarious.' But whatever her nagging doubts she tackled her task with the same determination which she brought to all her undertakings and tried to impose some order on the chaos. 'There are 42 children in the school. I wish they weren't so dirty; they *will* clean their slates by spitting on them and the girls afterwards rub theirs with their pinafores, which are also used as pocket handkerchiefs. Now that's *nasty*. Then all their clothes smell so strong in hot weather one can hardly stand it, moving about from child to child and leaning over them, or else sitting in the middle of 10 or 12 standing close round one reading.'

Yet in spite of her fastidious misgivings about the children's hygiene her role as schoolmarm gave her a kind of satisfaction that amounted almost to that of a mother with her brood: 'I took a little reading class then a big class and then a dictation class and finally let them sing one hymn. One feels wonderfully maternal sitting surrounded by a class of the smallest trying to read.' Nor was it only the children's backwardness and need that worried her. The whole village cried out to be cared for and nurtured by a volunteer who knew how to help raise it from its ignorance and neglect, a task well beyond her own capacity as a twenty-year-old upper-class girl from the fine mansion up the road. She asked plaintively: 'Why don't someone rise up with a vocation for Killay – I mean for doing what's wanted here. Someone is wanted to know Welsh and work hard and to know how to get hold of the people and keep the men from the public house by giving them some harmless and equally amusing place wherein to spend their evenings instead – and someone to teach well. In fact a volunteer Welsh genius is required but I'm afraid I don't see much chance of his turning up just at the moment.'

These larger philosophical considerations were often set aside when immediate practical assistance was needed. One day in 1866 an urgent message from Edward Brown, who had succeeded Montague Welby as Vicar of Sketty, informed Amy's father of a serious outbreak of cholera in Killay and she lost no time in offering what help she could.

At the Swansea Station Papa was met by a note from Mr Brown about the people by the Commercial Inn who had cholera, asking Papa to send them some beef tea and stuff so in the afternoon Papa went down to see the poor people. There is illness in two houses now; at one, the Rees's, the mother is still very ill but recovering; two children are also recovering and two are dead. At the other house, the Jenkins's, the father and mother are both very ill but the father is considered better. The mother is very ill indeed, far the worst of all I think. At both houses the only people in charge were one small girl about 16 or 18 years old. The one cottage is a real pig stye of a place – no wonder the cholera came there.

The following day saw her again setting off on her errand of mercy, laden with whatever provisions she thought necessary to relieve the suffering she saw all around her:

In the afternoon I went on a round of visits carrying chicken broth and jelly with me besides other victuals. At the Rees's I found the woman quite weak from fever – the consecutive fever they call it which follows cholera very often. But she was very weak and unable to eat. I gave her a few teaspoonfuls of the broth; the jelly was too sweet for her. Dr Williams (the local physician) amused me immensely when he found me in the Rees's cottage by putting on a severe face and telling me he considered it was very hazardous for me to be there.

The cholera epidemic of 1866 was one of the major outbreaks of the period – and fortunately for the poorest classes also one of the last of its kind – but Amy, who was well aware of the risk of infection, was not in the least intimidated by Dr Williams's stern warning. Wherever there was any kind of local tragedy or emergency or any old or neglected person who needed special care Amy Dillwyn would put on her stout walking-boots and bustle off with a basket of provisions, heedless of convention or fashion. With only the most rudimentary medical services to call on there was no one in Killay who would have scoffed at 'Lady Bountiful' on her charitable visits. After all any help was better than none, and the workmanlike Miss Dillwyn was not known for her condescension or hypocrisy. She was not a passive observer of the harrowing scenes of poverty and distress in the poorer districts, haughtily dispensing largesse as the lady of the manor; she worked tirelessly to nurse and comfort when she could without thought for her social position or her health. Being young and physically strong she rolled up her sleeves and set about her job like a professional, even commandeering medical luxuries from her father's resources at Hendrefoilan: 'In the morning I saw to the sending off of our air bed to lend to Mary Rees. In the afternoon Papa and I went on our round again with more chicken broth and beef tea. Mary Rees is slightly better; the daughter and I moved her on to the air bed I had sent down. She seemed to like it when on it but the exertion of being lifted on to it made her quite sick.'

Just after the worst of the cholera outbreak had died down Amy was again called into action when she heard of the plight of an old lady in Sketty called Betsy Lewis who was suffering from typhoid fever which like cholera was highly contagious. When she decided to go and visit Betsy she thought her father would be annoyed by her intervention, but in fact he was concerned enough to walk down with her when she took the invalid some beef tea and barley water. The old lady had been negligent in not paying her Clothing Club subscription and some of the local Ladies' Committee wanted to strike her off their list of worthy recipients, but Amy pleaded for her to be kept on the books a little longer and took her the rare treat of an orange which pleased poor Betsy immensely. When Betsy tried to thank her for her kindness Amy was as modest about her own role as ever and just as reluctant to respond to affection as she had always been.

> She paid me a high compliment when I went away saying 'Indeed Miss Dillwyn I do feel better since you've been in the room'. She's not given to pretty speeches much. No one ever said that to me before and it sounded pleasant enough certainly, tho' I daresay she didn't really mean it.

A few months later she called on another old lady, Mrs Isaacs, whose daughter had just lost her baby. Mrs Isaacs had heard that Miss Dillwyn was shortly leaving to go up to London for the Season and asked that she come to see her before she left Swansea. Describing her reaction to the scene in Mrs Isaacs's humble cottage Amy showed a profound sense of awe in the face of real tragedy and for once relaxed into open tenderness: 'The little child was lying on a table in the kitchen, tranquil and beautiful in its serenity and the quiet little face was wonderfully pretty, a very perfection of peace that no living face can ever approach to.' When Amy left the kitchen, her eyes moist with tears, 'the grandmother came outside the door with me and then in the dark she caught me in her arms round my waist and kissed my hand sobbing all the time. I suppose it was some kind of vent for her grief for I don't think she cares particularly about me.'

In incidents like these which involved the deepest human emotions the strict limits imposed on someone like Amy by her social position emerged very clearly. Genuinely engaged in her charitable work, in her 'poor peopling' as it was called at the time, she derived considerable satisfaction from actively helping to relieve distress. Yet she could not respond as a whole person to expressions of gratitude and even love from women below her on the social scale. She was never able to forget that she was 'Miss Dillwyn', the formidable young lady whose father was a prominent industrialist and politician. In no circumstances could she afford to unbend socially and reciprocate the feelings of those she helped, however strong the temptation to react sensitively to poor Mrs Isaacs's heartfelt sorrow: as a result her sense of isolation inevitably increased.

The gulf between the two nations of the rich and the poor, between the classes and the masses, was not easily bridged and she unwittingly recorded a notable example of its influence in an interesting account of an incident in the mid 1860s. One day she had been out riding in the country beyond Hendrefoilan and on the way home she witnessed a sight even then becoming fairly uncommon:

> I met a specimen of a genuine old Welsh funeral with some modern elements introduced; it was the funeral of Rosser the old farmer at the Goitree; first came about sixty or seventy men of the lower classes walking two-by-two; then a two-horse hearse and three mourning carriages (which part I considered as the modern elements) then one or two ordinary country people's carts, then a few more men and lastly a promiscuous crowd of women all dressed in their best clothes of whatever colour they might be. It was a curious assemblage and was the largest funeral of the kind I ever saw. As most of the men touched their hats to me I nearly nodded my head off before I got to the other end of the long line.

On the other hand, and in marked contrast to her own position, her brother Harry, totally gregarious and convivial to a fault, found it easy to mix with all classes of people. He was well known in Swansea for his heavy drinking and his easy manner and had few inhibitions about where he went or whom he met socially. The crucial difference, of course, was that he was a man. No respectable woman could have done what he did and still keep the reputation essential to a proper place in mid-Victorian society. Shrewd as she was Amy would not have missed the lesson to be learnt – that women were seldom treated fairly in a male-oriented world – and consequently her latent feminism began to grow stronger from this time onwards.

Gradually the experience which she gained in Killay taught her to challenge the validity of many taboos she might otherwise have taken for granted. It also taught her to assert, however tentatively at first, a woman's right to lead her own life even when that implied the right to choose whatever occupation or profession most suited her abilities. Much as she enjoyed the superficial charms of elegant living her innate Quakerism rebelled against idleness and the waste of human resources implicit in the stultifying etiquette of social calls and soirées.

As an ardently idealistic young woman in her twenties she looked at the upper-class world around her and was keenly dissatisfied with what she saw. 'There is so much work to do,' she wrote, 'and so many idle people in society who are doing nothing'. However hard she tried she found it almost impossible to see where she herself could fit into a social structure that was so rigidly predetermined. On a visit to London in the spring of 1869 she did her best to find voluntary work as a teacher in a church school in Kensington but, she commented, 'the present schoolmaster don't like ladies assisting in the boys' school, so I am again loose on the world and my services are available to anyone desiring them – but I'm afraid no one does – or if they do I don't know of them so I seem likely to remain idle. I wonder if I shall ever be in any way of use in the world. I suppose one wouldn't have been put into the world unless one was meant to fill some hole in it'.

But for the moment, even though she showed increasing awareness of the need to be doing something useful and rewarding, she had no alternative but to play a passive part as a member of the social élite, sharing her time between charity at home in Swansea and the idle pursuits of the glittering world of style and fashion in London.

Society and Suitors

Every year, as soon as she had done her duty in Swansea and Killay, Amy set off for London to carry out another and very different round of engagements. After her mother's premature death in 1866 she was, for all practical purposes, her father's hostess and partner and was therefore entitled to be asked to many social functions she would have had to forgo if her mother had still been alive. Lewis Dillwyn was a leading parliamentarian who, despite his radical politics, enjoyed good relations with the Prince of Wales and was often invited to royal 'drawing-rooms' to be received by the Queen in surroundings of great splendour. Whenever Amy was fortunate enough to accompany her father on these great ceremonial occasions she found the sense of sharing in a fairy-tale world almost irresistible. After one such encounter with royalty she wrote:

> I think Buckingham Palace a better place than St James's used to be; the rooms are larger and handsomer; it was very well arranged today so that there was no squash whatsoever and no need to stand all the time and plenty of seats. I do think a drawing room a very pretty sight; it is more like a picture of courts in the old days than anything else; there's every man and woman in their very best clothes, lace, jewellery, uniforms etc. and somehow most of us look better (I think) in full dress than in ordinary costume. I liked it very much.

In the summer of 1867 she and her father attended a great ball given at the India Office for the visiting Sultan of Turkey, which turned out to be a truly magnificent affair and one of the highlights of the Season. The evening's events were about as far removed from 'poor peopling' in Killay as it was possible to imagine, but Amy took it all in her stride with even a touch of poetry in her description of the scene:

> The ballroom was a large courtyard roofed over at the top so that it was the height of the whole building. The company was splendidly dressed and all the gentlemen were in uniform. A path was made when the Sultan arrived and very pretty the whole thing was when he walked up the path with Princess Alice on his arm, followed by the Prince of

Wales and the Duchess of Cambridge, Prince Louis of Hesse, Princess Mary and Prince Teck and their respective suites.

Dancing wasn't very furiously carried on by the general public who seemed to prefer thronging around where the Royal party danced and watching them. Of course the Grand Turk didn't dance but sat statelily and looked on until about 12½ when he went in to supper, again passing through (as it were) walls of ladies and gentlemen who divided for them and the other Royalties to pass and kept the path clear through the crowd. It is very pretty as Royalties pass through a crowd of that kind to see how every lady curtseys as they pass and every gentleman bows; it's like wind passing over corn, each head bends down and then comes up again while the bending movement is carried on without a break all down the line. I enjoyed seeing it all excessively though I didn't dance and we got home about 2½.

A few years later she and Essie went with their father to the opening concert at the newly built Albert Hall, only a stone's throw from their home in Knightsbridge, and again they revelled in the excitement of a social occasion which attracted all the celebrities of the day, including the Queen herself and her new son-in-law the Marquis of Lorne who had just married the Princess Louise.

We had excellent places in a box and heard everything very well indeed. Disraeli and Lady Beaconsfield were in the next box to us, but of course Lord Lorne was *the* great attraction to us as we had not seen him before. The Queen is certainly very plain but she has an excellent voice and the few words she said were audible over the whole building. The Prince of Wales has got very bald.

Because her father was one of Gladstone's most faithful supporters among the Radical group in the House of Commons, Amy was also given the opportunity of mixing in some of the highest political circles in London. When Benjamin Disraeli became Prime Minister for a brief period in the winter of 1868 Lewis Dillwyn was invited to a great celebration party at the Foreign Office presided over by the elderly and ailing Mrs Disraeli. Unfortunately his eccentric hostess omitted to invite Dillwyn's daughter who was very much put out by the oversight. 'Mrs Disraeli has been neglectful enough not to include me also', commented Amy who had never entertained a very high opinion of the new Premier and his wife. However, after

Gladstone had roundly defeated Disraeli in the general election of 1868 the new Foreign Secretary, the Earl of Clarendon, gave an equally glittering Foreign Office reception at which Amy was flattered to find herself among the distinguished guests and even more gratified to meet the most dominant figure in Victorian politics. The faintly ironic tone of her account hardly disguises her genuine pleasure in speaking to such a celebrity:

> Tonight Papa and I went to Lady Clarendon's reception at the Foreign Office which was a very pretty sight and where we met heaps of friends and then went on to Mrs Gladstone's 'At Home'. I was introduced to Mr Gladstone and had the felicity of shaking hands with the great man.

Royalty and statesmen apart, Amy was possibly even more pleased to meet men who had made their mark purely by their intellectual merit – the novelists, artists, poets and philosophers whose work gave them the entrée to 'the best circles' in London Society. As she moved through the palatial drawing-rooms of Belgravia Amy encountered not only great wealth but also great intellect. Men like Robert Browning, James Antony Froude the eminent historian, Thomas Hughes (of *Tom Brown's Schooldays*), and William Makepeace Thackeray stimulated her mind as powerfully as Royalty and nobility stimulated her sense of colour and romance.

One evening she was taken down to dinner on the arm of Auberon Herbert, younger son of the Earl of Carnarvon, and a Liberal MP of advanced radical and republican views. Herbert, still a bachelor and only a little older than Amy, was a marvellously interesting companion for a young woman longing for an opportunity of broadening her horizons:

> I was very glad to meet Mr Herbert as one always is to meet a man who is at all celebrated in any way. He talked a great deal about the education of both men and women and then went off into what he believed in religious matters. I can't say I like talking religion in general society but still his views had a considerable interest in them. The fact of his being a man who is clever and rather original made me curious to hear what he said on the subject.

While talking to such a man she ignored his reputation as a daring radical, simply letting her intelligence come to terms with new ideas and original theories. She had read with great interest some of the writing of John Stuart Mill who had done more than anyone to campaign for the rights of women, and in the company of men like Herbert she recognized how much she had lost by not having had the opportunity of a university education.

At this period the Oxford and Cambridge colleges were only just beginning to open their doors to women and Amy was by then too mature a student to become one of Tennyson's 'sweet girl graduates'. One of the few avenues open to her was music, a constant source of emotional and intellectual satisfaction, and in order to pursue her musical interests more seriously she persuaded her father to engage as her tutor the services of John Goss, one of the most talented musicians in London.

Goss was the organist of St Paul's Cathedral and Professor of Harmony at the Royal College of Music. He had been a pupil of Mozart's protegé, Thomas Attwood, and had composed tunes for such well-known hymns as 'Praise my Soul the King of Heaven' and 'In the Bleak Mid-Winter'. For a modest fee of fourteen shillings a lesson he sat down with Amy and tried to teach her the intricacies of harmony and counterpoint; but, despite his reputation, Amy found him an unrewarding teacher just as he seems to have found her a fairly recalcitrant pupil. He wanted to talk, and she wanted to learn.

> Had a lesson from Goss this morning who stayed almost two hours and didn't work for one. He is such an inveterate talker and digresses and digresses until it's a wonder how he ever does anything. I don't think he and I ever have the same idea regarding words to be set to music.

By an ironic coincidence one of the pieces of poetry she especially admired was destined to become a classic in the hands of a composer more gifted than either Goss or herself. Reading the poems of Adelaide Proctor she wrote: 'I admire "The Lost Chord" uncommonly and kept setting it to music in my head all the time, which was very amusing.' Just ten years later, Arthur Sullivan, Goss's most famous pupil, made that same poem one of the most popular items in the whole repertoire of Victorian popular song.

But as was often the case with Amy's high-flying ideas her ambition outstripped her achievement and her rueful self-mocking sense of humour kept breaking through her delusions of intellectual grandeur. On hearing of the death of Rossini, for instance, she confessed to herself: 'If I could only write music like him I should be happy. Oh! to think how far removed I am from such geniuses − but still I would put up with being a genius of any kind!'

The major difference between an acknowledged genius like Rossini or, at another level, Sullivan, and someone like Amy was that men were able to pursue their musical studies as a serious profession whereas it was considered that a woman could only dabble in music as a pastime or amusement. It was precisely this lack of systematic training, so deplored by radical thinkers like Florence Nightingale, that disqualified Amy from even attempting a musical career, and enabled Goss to treat her as a mere amateur with nothing better to do. And of course Goss was essentially right. As a rule young women in Amy's position did not have anything better to do nor were they ever encouraged to do anything other than move as decoratively as possible through 'Society'. Inevitably, therefore, keeping up with the latest fashion was regarded as more appropriate for the average young girl than pursuing intellectual ideas or seeking a formal education.

After one excursion in search of new clothes Amy commented: 'Amongst other things I bought a new bonnet which has an ornament behind that I find is called "Suivez-moi jeune homme". Certainly people do give things quaint names.' Time and again she wavers between a full-hearted enjoyment of the material pleasures of life, like jewellery and fine clothes, and a slightly puritanical distaste for such frivolous luxuries. The truth was that she was still only in her mid-twenties with several years of opportunity for marriage before she reached the crucial age of thirty, generally regarded as the time in a girl's life when spinsterhood was almost inevitable. She was still open to offers even from eligible bachelors in Swansea but she nevertheless resolutely refused the most consistent (or persistent) of her local admirers, the Reverend Edward Bolney, vicar of her parish church at Sketty.

The vicar had been born Edward Brown but had taken his new surname from an aunt who had left him a legacy on condition he changed from Brown to Bolney. From the time he first succeeded her uncle Montague Welby as incumbent, Bolney had been less than popular with Amy. At first she simply disapproved of the way he read the lessons in church, suggesting that he should intone them in the proper Church of England manner rather than mumble them into his full set of whiskers. He obviously took this advice to heart since he was remembered for this very quality many years afterwards. However, when he began to pay her personal attention Amy became alarmed and annoyed.

One Sunday morning in the winter of 1870 after she had listened to the Sketty Church choir singing a tune she had written for 'Thou art Weary' she returned home to find that Bolney's sister Miss Brown had delivered a message from her brother asking to see Miss Dillwyn alone. She immediately conferred with her companion and chaperone Miss Buller and 'we agree that it sounds most suspiciously like a proposal and as I have not the slightest desire for that Miss Buller has written to say I don't wish to see him, and I'm sure we shan't hear any more about it'. But she was wrong. A few days afterwards the hapless clergyman tried again more directly: 'First thing at breakfast I had the felicity of receiving a long letter from Mr Bolney containing an offer in form! And after I had trusted Miss Buller's letter had quenched him! It was an aggravation & made me ferocious. I sent him as decided and unqualified a refusal as Miss Buller, Harry and I between us could concoct so now I do hope it's ended.'

Four years later Parson Bolney wrote again repeating his request for an interview and she had once more to repel his advances: 'What an awful bore it is! I do think he might have known I didn't like him and have taken up with someone else in all this time. But it *is* a bore and no mistake.' Even when she approached the perilous age of thirty she continued to decline offers which she did not find attractive. In the autumn of 1874 she found yet another letter from the vicar lying on her table but by this time she regarded him as slightly dotty and let the matter rest: 'After his having written the other day to say that as long as I remain single he would do the same he now writes to ask that in spite of all that is passed he and I should remain on terms of friendship and freely discuss all Killay matters together! Really I think he must be mad.'

From his own point of view Bolney was by no means mad, though he was certainly insensitive and unwise. Cambridge educated, comfortably off and widely respected by his parishioners, he saw no reason why he should not ask Miss Amy Dillwyn of Hendrefoilan House to become his soulmate in the Church to which they were both devoted. He knew that Amy's Aunt Mary had only recently married his predecessor Welby and was then living quite contentedly as the vicar's wife, dispensing charity and good works at Oystermouth Church. Unfortunately for him Amy was not only much younger than her aunt had been when she married but also far more emancipated in her ideas. Having mixed with profoundly interesting and unorthodox men like Froude and Auberon Herbert in the highest echelons of London society, and having absorbed herself in reading original thinkers as diverse as Pusey and John Stuart Mill she had no intention of becoming a vicar's lady like Aunt Mary, dedicated to Sunday School teaching at Killay and serving gruel to the poor.

Leaving the persistent parson aside Amy's view of the clergy as a whole was far from flattering. She valued their spiritual role but found the men themselves, like her cousin Weston Moggridge or Edward Bolney, generally disappointing and not a little dull. Just at this period she accepted a dinner invitation to a smart house in London on a very special day in the social calendar. 'I was sent down to dinner with a clergyman which I thought hard lines as "Have you been to the Derby?" was the natural commencement to dinner conversation on this – the Derby day – and of course one could not propound *that* to a clergyman!'

This constant tug-of-war between the devout young church-goer and the gay young thing can best be seen in her ambivalent attitude to women of the world who were brave enough to scorn polite society altogether, whatever the social consequences. One day while strolling in Hyde Park with her father she indulged in an admiring fashion note on an extremely fashionable lady:

> There has been a change since the long trains sweeping the ground last year. I didn't see one today; everyone wore a short gown or else had their dress looped up. I think Lady Cardigan was one of the best dressed of the walkers. Short black velvet gown, black velvet jacket with tight band round the waist, red petticoat, black bonnet with one red flower. Boots with very high heels coming to an absolute point and a rosary and cross hanging from her waist that clinked at every step. One couldn't help noticing her especially because she walks so well.

Adeline, Lady Cardigan, had just lost her husband, the highly controversial leader of the Charge of the Light Brigade at Balaclava, with whom she had openly lived in sin while his first wife was still alive. Ostracized by the Queen and by most polite hostesses she delighted in riding and walking in the Park wearing eye-catching clothes, confident enough in her wealth and aristocratic arrogance to ignore the quizzical glances of more reputable women. Amy would have been well aware of Lady Cardigan's notoriety but was so obviously impressed by the style as to overlook the dubious nature of the content. Here was a woman bold and beautiful enough to defy convention, and so strong willed that she could afford to follow her whims and desires as she pleased without constantly looking over her shoulder to see if 'the world' approved her conduct. Like Amy she, too, was destined to live to a great age and never ceased to shock her more staid contemporaries.

Moral Amazons

Such encounters with ladies of equivocal reputation like the Countess of Cardigan set Amy thinking about her own style of life and the crippling limitations which society imposed on women in her position.

> I wish I didn't like the world of pleasure and self-pleasing so much, or if so didn't think it right for me to give them up. It does seem so pleasant to let things go on naturally and take all the pleasures and enjoyments that seem to come as easily as the air we breathe. And it seems as if it couldn't be so very wrong when so many people go on doing it. It's very trying to see other people, and good people too, who go on taking life as it comes and honestly doing their duties while also enjoying the pleasures of the world . . .

This is Amy 'speculating' for all she is worth, wrestling with various forces pulling at her as she attempts to reconcile her natural desires with her spiritual aspirations. She was young, active and full of life but constantly controlled her love of fun and pleasure in case she fell into the cardinal sin of self-indulgence. All through her life she clung to the concept of 'duty' as the basis of human conduct; but she was human enough to want to lay down the burden and live like other 'ordinary' people with all their affectations and weaknesses. After the shock of losing Llewellyn and especially since the long days and nights when she had nursed her mother through her last illness Amy was deeply aware of the conflict between duty and pleasure.

Sitting down one day to read her favourite magazine, the *Cornhill*, she found a story by Thackeray's daughter Anne called 'The Village on the Cliff' which touched a sensitive and responsive chord. Anne Thackeray wrote of two types of women, the soft vulnerable girl who sought and aroused the protective instinct in a man, and the apparently tough and self-sufficient woman who often seemed to scorn love and affection but secretly yearned for someone to break down her hard shell: 'The strongest and fiercest of amazons would be glad to lay down her arms at times and rest and be weak and cared for; but the help comes not for her (as for women of weaker mould and nature) — she must bear the burden of her strength and courage and fight on until the night.' Anne Thackeray, like Amy, had lost her mother and been obliged to look after a father who had taken her supportive role very much for granted, without realizing what a heavy burden of self-sacrifice he had imposed on his dutiful daughter. Thackeray's Anne and Lewis Dillwyn's Amy had much in common. Amy's comment was heartfelt: 'I especially agree in one little bit about there being moral amazons among women in the world and that these amazons sometimes wish to lay aside their strength and love and be loved and cared for like other women, but in vain; the amazon must pay the penalty of her strength and suffer for the respect paid to her.'

Being herself a striking example of one of those 'moral amazons' Amy was only too well aware of how easy life could be for 'women of weaker mould and nature'. Her younger sister Essie was a perfect example of the weaker woman, spoilt and helpless yet seemingly capable of inspiring the love and admiration often denied to girls obliged to stand on their own two feet as Amy was, without a husband or a lover.

Just when the family had recovered from the loss of Bessie Dillwyn and achieved a kind of equilibrium under Amy's stewardship, she realized that Essie had found a suitor. Essie's engagement, though entirely natural and not unexpected, was an agonizing time for Amy because it strengthened her own feelings of failure and isolation. If life had gone according to plan it would have been Amy's turn to follow Minnie up the aisle of Sketty Church on her bridegroom's arm, not Essie's who was so much younger and so much less deserving. But that was not to be.

In the summer of 1872 Essie had met a young man named Fulwar Craven, a dark, good-looking Captain in the Grenadier Guards whose grandfather, also Fulwar Craven, had been a noted character on the turf in the 1830s and 40s, winning the Oaks with his horse 'Deception' in 1839. Fulwar's father, Goodwin Colquitt-Craven, travelled up from his home at Brockhampton Park, near Cheltenham, in August to see Lewis Dillwyn about the details of a marriage settlement for Essie. As soon as this had been completed, by Essie's father settling the sum of £6000 upon her, Fulwar came to Hendrefoilan to propose formally to Essie and was accepted by her, the wedding being fixed for early the following year.

Whereas such an engagement would normally have given great cause for satisfaction, Amy was almost driven to distraction by envy, grief and disappointment. To see Essie – silly, vain, frivolous Essie, so much younger and so much the family favourite – engaged to be married to her handsome Captain while Amy still languished at home was a truly savage blow. Amy said nothing openly but in the privacy of her diary she almost broke her heart, stunned by the sheer unfairness of it all. For once self-pity almost overwhelmed her stoicism. 'Hendrefoilan looks so pretty and peaceful tonight that I feel as though it were almost a sin to bring such a weary, and I sometimes think, half-broken heart as mine into so beautiful a place. How little does the world or one's own family or anyone except oneself know the bitterness of one's own heart! And how little do they suspect it either.'

As she sat down to write all the letters announcing Essie's engagement she was consumed with jealousy. 'Essie spent the day with her beloved Fulwar – seeming to have neither eyes, ears nor thought for anyone or anything else. Of course, it's the natural order of things and was to be expected but all the same it's a little hard to find oneself so utterly and completely put to the wall for an untried stranger. Why am I never to have the happiness of loving and being loved? Am I worse natured than other people that my life must be so much bitterer than theirs? I cannot go on living like this.' On the following Sunday she went to morning service at Sketty Church as usual 'but as most of the time was spent in trying to keep from crying I should doubt whether I profited much from it'.

Nevertheless she tried to do her best when a few months later she was obliged to act as one of Essie's eight bridesmaids at what was Swansea's wedding of the year. The 'wedding invasion', as she wryly called it, began a week before the ceremony with relations and friends arriving at Hendrefoilan in droves, including the bridegroom's loquacious mother Mrs Georgina Craven. With only a few brief comments to herself, 'I should like it if this week were over – Mrs Craven never stops talking and I'm getting a sight of stuff poured into my ears', Amy composed herself and gave up her mornings to ticketing and setting out the wedding presents which were pouring in.

Thursday, 23 January 1873 was the wedding day. The church at Sketty was packed with well-wishers, the weather was fine and at 11.30 in the morning the guard of honour from various battalions of the Glamorgan Rifle Volunteer Corps was drawn up at the pretty lychgate to welcome Captain Craven and his bride, while the band of the Corps performed a choice selection of music against the pealing of the bells. Essie wore a rich white *poult-de-soie* dress trimmed with white satin, Brussels lace, and flounces looped with bouquets of orange flowers. Her neck was adorned with an exquisitely-designed gold necklace with a locket attached and which was mounted with diamonds, rubies and pearls. Amy like the other seven bridesmaids was attired in white grenadine over a white silk dress trimmed with cerise and sage green, with a head-dress of azaleas and a tulle veil. The press reporters on the scene were lyrical in their long descriptions of what had all the hallmarks of a highly auspicious occasion, and their accounts included half a column of print devoted to the gifts lavished on the happy pair. The cream of Glamorganshire society was present to honour the young daughter of Swansea's widely respected Member of Parliament, with the Talbots, the Nicholls, the Hicks-Beaches and the Dillwyn Llewelyns leading the way.

By half-past three in the afternoon it was all over and Essie and Fulwar were *en route* for their honeymoon in Rome leaving Hendrefoilan in a shower of slippers and rice. After their departure the Dillwyn family and their principal guests drove down to Killay schoolroom where there was a party for the children and where a good time was had by all, except the bride's still unmarried sister. Chief bridesmaid Amy says nothing of the ceremony in her diary which simply records the fact that it had taken place, and where one might expect a page of colourful comment there is only: 'Essie's wedding day and now she is Mrs Fulwar Craven. It seems hardly possible to realise it and yet there seems a desolate blank in the house. Essie and Fulwar get to Gloucester tonight.' As she sat in her bedroom writing that bleak record, thinking of the happy honeymoon couple at Gloucester and miserably comparing her sister's fate with her own, she knew real despair for perhaps the first time in her life.

Amy in the Literary World

With Essie successfully married Amy was faced with the problem of her own role in society. Approaching thirty without a mother to act as matchmaker and with a father and brother who preferred their own country pursuits to the frivolities of town life, she now had no real function. To continue the social round, with regular visits to London for the Season at one end of the scale and charitable good works in Swansea at the other, now seemed pointless and increasingly embarrassing to a woman no longer young and scarcely eligible for a suitable marriage. Amy thus realized that the pursuit of such a purposeless routine was no more than an expensive waste of time, and rather than continue with the same lifestyle she fell back, as did many Victorian spinsters, on the excuse of invalidism. For whatever reason, she began actually to feel that her health had failed and this gave her the perfect pretext for opting out of the social commitments she had hitherto enjoyed.

As the 1870s wore on she found her physical condition deteriorating to the point where she hardly ever went out and spent most of her time at Hendrefoilan reading and dreaming, describing herself as being 'stuck to the sofa like a limpet on a rock'. The cause of her illness is hard to determine and she herself could hardly account for it though she acknowledged by implication that it was probably as psychosomatic in origin as that of her great contemporary Florence Nightingale. Miss Nightingale, too, had been overendowed with intelligence and underendowed with the means of applying that intelligence to some useful purpose, at least until the war in the Crimea gave her the opening she needed. There was no such 'calling' to tempt Amy into public life but there was the world of literary endeavour and, being confined to her couch, she had plenty of time to try her hand at writing a novel. She may have become a limpet but at least she could be a literary limpet and put her reading and dreaming to some use.

Her first reference to actually writing novels rather than endlessly reading them occurs interestingly enough just after it had become clear that Essie's marriage was a certainty. Almost as a reaction to this bitter blow Amy decided to work out her frustrated feelings in the form of fiction. 'I've an idea I will try and write one chapter of a novel and then see how I like it' but as she freely confessed: 'I haven't any genius for literature or literary composition and only take to it as a *pis-aller*, using my brains because I can't use my muscles, which last I should greatly prefer.' Despite this modest disclaimer she did in fact write rather well and her novels of the 1880s are still worth reading even if her fiction is seldom as interesting as her diaries where the real woman is allowed far more emotional release than any of her fictional heroines.

She had already tried her hand at writing short stories and religious allegories but these were small-scale affairs doomed either to rejection from the publishers or instant obscurity. And having just read and greatly admired George Eliot's masterpiece, *Middlemarch*, Amy was determined to write a real novel about real people and not merely religious tales for children. She was self-critical enough to know that she could not hope to rival a writer like Eliot whose intellect outstripped that of almost any woman of the period, but she could at least compete for attention with some of the popular novelists of the day and that is exactly what she succeeded in doing. To say that her novels are now forgotten should be considered alongside the fact that most of her rivals have suffered a similar fate, many of them, such as Margaret Oliphant or Rhoda Broughton, far more famous than she was in their own time.

Her first attempt, as she had anticipated, was an abject failure reported with her usual realism. One Monday morning she wrote 'I took my novel to Hurst & Blackett the publishers with the absolute knowledge that it's rubbish and not worth publishing'. On the following Wednesday she conceded: 'my estimate of my novel was confirmed by Messrs Hurst & Blackett'. The speedy confirmation of her misgivings says much both for her critical faculty and the admirable promptitude of Victorian publishers, but she was not easily deterred and doggedly went on with her writing.

It was not until 1880 that her persistence was finally rewarded with the publication by Macmillan of a new novel *The Rebecca Rioter* 'by E. A. Dillwyn'. The impersonal initials on the title page may have been the result of her desire not to be regarded as yet another genteel lady novelist and the book gives very few clues to the sex of the author. Her success in finding a publisher may have owed something to her father's social acquaintance with the head of the firm, Alexander Macmillan, who perhaps eased the difficulties usually met by the average aspiring writer from the provinces; but the story was a good one and well deserved its appearance in print. Her father was also helpful in providing her with a theme because he himself had a vivid personal recollection of the Rebecca Riots some forty years earlier and had in fact written an exciting account of his involvement with the raids on the Pontarddulais toll-gate just outside Swansea.

In 1880 the Rebecca Riots were just beginning to fade from public memory, and this 'story of Killay life', as Amy called it, needed the stimulus of her father's first-hand experience to bring it to life. As previously mentioned, Lewis Dillwyn and his brother John Dillwyn Llewelyn of Penllergaer, in their capacity as county magistrates, had been instrumental in putting down the destructive attacks on the toll-gates of south-west Wales, though both were liberal enough to acknowledge the basic justice of the rioters' case. Indeed both of them had called for leniency in dealing with 'the daughters of Rebecca' whom they had personally apprehended after a fierce hand-to-hand skirmish. With all this background material in the family records Amy could scarcely fail to write a rattling good tale and *The Rebecca Rioter* is precisely that. She made the most of a golden opportunity and wrote a highly readable novel.

Having achieved a successful literary debut Amy felt secure enough as a novelist to look beyond her home ground and to attempt a novel called *Chloe Arguelle* based on her own experience of life in London. On her father's copy of the novel she carefully inked in her own hand the subtitle 'Caricatures of the Humbugs' making it perfectly clear that her own view of London society was by no means that of the conventional romantic writer. There is nothing in this book of the fairy-tale splendour which had often impressed her as a young debutante, only quiet scorn both for the army of poseurs and frauds who haunted fashionable drawing-rooms and for the religious hypocrites who condemned Sunday amusements for the masses while carefully ensuring that their own private pleasures were not interfered with. She shows an almost Dickensian contempt for anything sanctimonious and false, and she also shares Dickens's weakness for the sensational. Like all her later novels *Chloe Arguelle* ends with a melodramatic flourish in which the family butler murders not only his master but also the daughter of the household while the heroine Chloe marries her hero to inaugurate a joint 'crusade against humbug!'

This crusading theme of social reform lies at the heart of all six of the novels which make up the bulk of Amy's literary work during her productive decade from 1880 to the early 1890s. All the stories are autobiographical in so far as they deal daringly with the plight of highly intelligent women who cannot find a truly useful and rewarding place in a conventional society dominated by men. Like Amy herself the heroines are seldom beautiful and have no time for simpering mannerisms and feminine naïvety. They are often tomboys with a robust sense of fun and invariably courageous enough to defend their unorthodox attitudes in the face of every kind of opposition and prejudice. Their personal rebelliousness never involves any suggestion of sexual nonconformity, indeed they are strenuously virtuous, but they show a stubborn refusal to be used by men as decorative ornaments, to become mere dolls in a doll's house. Amy was writing in the same period as Ibsen and Shaw and was fully aware of the growing movement towards female equality among the newly-emancipated women of the middle and upper classes.

In order to draw attention to the widespread suppression of women in every walk of life she chose some radically original themes. The heroine of her third novel *A Burglary* belies the Victorian stereotyped girl to the extent of refusing a very eligible suitor (until virtually the end of the book) simply because she does not wish to marry for the sake of marrying. As a reviewer in the *Spectator* acknowledged in his appraisal of what he called an unhackneyed and refreshing novel 'there is a good deal of humour in Miss Dillwyn, even a touch of Miss Austen'. The flattering comparison was not quite as exaggerated as it may seem when it is remembered that both women shared the same cool detached view of the follies of a world which had denied them husbands and granted marital status to frivolous girls with nothing to recommend them but a fortune and superficial good looks.

There is not the slightest touch of Jane Austen in Amy's fourth novel *Jill* which was closely followed by a sequel called *Jill and Jack*. Here Amy allows free expression to her social radicalism by permitting Jill, her well-born protagonist, to become a lady's maid who stoops as low as fraud and theft to revenge herself against a father who remarries and leaves her penniless. Renouncing 'England that abode of Snobs' with its odious title-worshippers Jill travels abroad in her role as a humble servant in search of a new life and vigorously resists all attempts on her virtue, as a 'new woman' should.

In one splendid scene Amy demonstrates how well she could write when she describes how Jill deals with the advances of a fellow employee who presumes to kiss her against her will. Perkins the would-be seducer is a vulgar valet who wastes no time with gallantries or finesse. He seizes Jill in his arms and 'leering detestably' tries to embrace her assuming, as such a man would, that the only reason for her reluctance is her fear of being seen: 'there's no one looking so you needn't purtend not to like it'. Faced by such villainous behaviour Jill does exactly what Amy would have done in similar circumstances: she grabs a lighted candle and thrusts it in the odious Perkins's face with dire results for his appearance. 'In another instant there was a strong smell of burning hair and one of his cherished whiskers was on fire.' When next seen the scoundrel had paid a public price for his audacity. 'The hairy appendages to his face, in which he delighted, were gone for the whisker I had set on fire had been so much destroyed that it had to be shaved off, and then of course its companion had been obliged to follow suit.' The reviewer of *Jill* in the *Spectator* was so struck by this outstanding example of defiant womanhood that he devoted a whole column of quotation to the singeing of Perkins's whiskers as a grim warning to men who tried to take advantage of not-so-defenceless women. Amy had made her point amusingly but the serious message was unmistakable: girls would no longer tolerate male exploitation be it valets abusing maids or husbands ill-treating their wives.

Determined to strike a blow for female emancipation Amy was not above using either knockabout comedy or sheer melodrama as weapons in her literary armoury. She was, however, aware of the pitfalls of too much propaganda and lightened her solemn moments with humour, as when she describes Jill's future husband Jack as 'belonging to the class of country gentlemen who likes the world to be aired for them by other people before they make their appearance in it', and when she reprimands those vain women who spend ages titivating themselves before receiving long-expected guests: 'Making oneself extra gorgeous whilst their visitors are kicking their heels waiting – I do call that such nonsense! If clothes are so untidy that one's ashamed to be seen in them, then they're too untidy to be worn about the house at all.'

Since she was exploiting the current vogue for 'daring' fiction, made enormously popular by best-sellers like Mary Elizabeth Braddon and Rhoda Broughton, she liberally sprinkled her plots with burglaries, disastrous fires, and horrendous murders as well as a spice of racy slang for good measure. Her villains are described as 'sloping off with all the tin they could lay their hands on for a moonlight flitting' when they have no option but to 'skedaddle'. She writes of refrigerators and frozen food, of people using the telephone and turning on the electric light; and there is a surprising modernity about Amy's fiction which seems to belie the high-Victorian period in which her novels are firmly set.

While she was consolidating her position as a minor novelist during the 1880s Amy was also a regular contributor to the *Spectator*, a weekly paper which then enjoyed a wide readership among the educated classes. Its distinguished editor Richard Holt Hutton was a close friend of her father's (they frequently played chess together at the Athenaeum) and Lewis Dillwyn persuaded Hutton to include Amy on his panel of reviewers. For more than ten years she received regular boxes of books from London and produced something like sixty articles, chiefly reviews of contemporary fiction but also a wide variety of general works, all of them filled with her own brand of sound common-sense. Since the reviews were published anonymously she did not gain much public prestige for her work in the *Spectator*, but she did receive the fairly handsome fee of five guineas for each article and had the considerable satisfaction of seeing her work in print in a reputable journal.

One of her most perceptive reviews (and the one of which she was most proud) appeared in 1884. One day in March she opened her parcel of books and found a copy of Robert Louis Stevenson's *Treasure Island* which had just been published for the first time in volume form. She immediately recognized its classic quality and took it to her father for a second opinion. In her review she awarded the highest praise she could muster to Jim Hawkins and the company of the *Hispaniolq*, enlisting her father as a disinterested critic of this children's book *par excellence*.

> We may mention having seen a gentleman take the book and at once become so absorbed that hardly a word could be got out of him and that he put it down not at all till he got to the end, except for the necessary purpose of luncheon; yet he is no boy or person of childish intellect but a man of business and science, and the chairman of an important manufacturing company.

One of the reasons she gave for her warm admiration of *Treasure Island* was so typical of Amy's no-nonsense approach to literature that it deserves to be quoted in full: 'By-the-bye it is worthy of note that the only female character is Jim's mother – who might just as well have belonged to the other sex for all she had to do – and that there is not a vestige of love-making in the whole book. Does not this refute the commonly received theory of the tender passion being indispensable in order to make a story amusing?'

In later years the popular press often credited Amy with having been the first to discover the adult merits of Stevenson's classic story for children. Sometimes she even made such a claim to enquiring newspaper reporters, though generally with her tongue in her cheek as she knew that other reviewers had been equally laudatory.

If her appreciation of *Treasure Island* was one of the most perceptive examples of Amy's literary criticism then the review she published a few weeks later was surely one of the most extraordinary. Hutton had sent her a book by the Welsh-American writer William Dean Howells then at the height of his fame as a realistic novelist. His latest novel, *A Woman's Reason*, caught Amy's imagination because it concerned a young Bostonian called Helen Harkness whose father dies suddenly and leaves her penniless as a result of his business failures. Plunged into instant poverty and forced out of her home she faces the choice of either asking friends and relatives for charity or going out to find work. Too proud to seek assistance Helen moves into cheap lodgings and begins her battle for independence in a world hostile to the very idea of female equality. After two years of hard toil which includes turning out literary reviews she finally overcomes her difficulties and accepts her new role in life: 'I have got to working at last as other people do who earn their own living.'

Howells changes tack at the end of the novel and rescues Helen from her problems by the familiar device of a good marriage but despite his avoidance of the crucial issues the lesson to be drawn from the story is quite clear. Amy pointed out that such a simplistic solution 'will seem shocking to advocates of female independence and the equality of men and women' because there was no good reason, other than male prejudice, why women should not stand on their own feet financially. When she sat down in the security of Hendrefoilan House to write her review of Howells's novel Amy had no inkling of how prophetic this book would turn out to be in her own life, but the seeds of her future salvation must have been sown in her mind; it *was* possible for a well-born woman to leave her gilded cage and fly freely in her own world asking favours of no man.

Although she hardly realized it at the time, Amy's literary work was much more than the hobby she had originally thought it to be. As her new career as novelist and reviewer advanced she gained not only a certain status and confidence as a woman of letters but also strengthened her own intellectual development. During this 'literary' phase of her life she had both the time and the medium in which to crystallize and express the feminist ideas with which she had previously only toyed, and she soon began to interpret life and society in a way that was peculiarly her own. No longer distracted by the pleasures of the great and glittering world of Victorian high society, and deprived of the chance of marriage and thus of a family of her own she became sceptical and disillusioned about the shallowness of fashionable life based only on the 'marriage market'. She retreated to the comfortable isolation of Hendrefoilan and distilled her experiences in a series of novels that were basically variations on a single theme: women ought not to be content to remain mere possessions of men but should assert themselves as intelligent human beings.

By writing these novels she germinated ideas that were soon to come to fruition in a way she could never have contemplated. Her fiction was a preparation for the actual challenges which were shortly to come her way and to change her whole life. It was, however, only a really traumatic series of events that could release her from the protective shell of vaguely defined ill health that for the moment held her 'like a limpet on a rock'.

Catastrophe and Salvation

Strangely enough it was the much-envied Essie who began the series of setbacks which brought Amy her salvation, her blessing in disguise. Essie's marriage in 1873 appeared to have been altogether successful. She and Fulwar Craven had set up home at Brockhampton Park and soon had a large and seemingly happy family consisting of three boys and two girls. But after thirteen years of decent wedlock, Mrs Fulwar Craven met a handsome young actor from Cheltenham called Richard Pakenham, fell hopelessly in love and eventually eloped with him to South Africa, leaving poor Fulwar with five motherless children.

Absolutely astounded by what had happened Amy sat down on 19 February 1886 to tell 'Dearest Minnie' the appalling news of their sister's desertion of her young family:

> Alas! it is all quite true. Fulwar and Harry are doing all they can to trace Essie and have employed a detective. Harry says the man is a penniless scamp with a good voice, a sort of second-class Cheltenham snob with no character and who will certainly desert her and turn her adrift when it suits him to do so. It is the most awful and horrible thing that has ever yet happened to me in all my life and I can do hardly anything but think about it. Oh, if we can only save her! anyhow, or somehow! She has taken with her photographs of all the children which she had on her bedroom table when here in Hendrefoilan.

Harry who loved Essie's children and who, despite his heavy drinking, was a stickler for propriety used all his experience as a barrister to try and return his wayward sister to the bosom of her family. Far from well and ageing rapidly as a result of his self-neglect Harry took it upon himself, a lifelong bachelor, to help Fulwar Craven look after the abandoned children and to guide the family through the inevitable divorce proceedings. Not long after the elopement he had arranged to meet Essie in London and found her quite unrepentant, even defiant, as he reported to Minnie in his usual down-to-earth manner:

> She came to meet me here at the station, not to see me, not to send a message to her children, but only to ask me to try to prevent criminal

proceedings against her 'dear Dick', threatening suicide if there should be any. She nearly made me sick. I told her that if I did as *I* wished I should like to give 'dear Dick' twelve months hard labour, kick him when he came out, and shoot him afterwards, and if I did not it was because of increasing the scandal.

Amy was so determined to rescue Essie from the trap into which she had fallen that she even followed her to South Africa in an effort to bring her errant sister back home. After a long and gruelling voyage to Cape Town in the winter of 1887, accompanied only by her maid, Amy found that Essie actually intended to marry her 'dear Dick' and was quite adamant that she would continue to share his precarious existence as a touring player. Realizing that there was nothing more to be done Amy was obliged to turn around almost as soon as she had arrived and take the boat back to England, not for the first time absolutely thwarted by Essie's stubborn insistence on having her own way.

As a result Harry and Amy were left with the problem of a broken-hearted husband drowning his sorrows in strong drink, and five children to be cared for. Harry, to his great credit, spent much of his time acting as a substitute parent at Brockhampton Park and calling on Amy's assistance whenever he could knowing that she, too, had her hands full looking after their father whose health and mental faculties were steadily failing after a severe fall which had temporarily deprived him of his reason. Even if she had been free Amy could not have moved into Brockhampton while Fulwar Craven was still there because to do so would have been quite improper for a maiden lady in her position. There had been scandal enough.

By the beginning of the 1890s both Fulwar Craven and Harry were drinking themselves literally to death and Amy's fortunes were at their lowest ebb. When Harry died in April 1890, still only 46, she recognized that her troubles were only just beginning since her brother's death meant that she could no longer look forward to spending the rest of her life with him at Hendrefoilan. By Harry's will the house was left to the next male heir (who was Minnie's eldest son John Iltyd Dillwyn Nicholl) with his father Lewis Dillwyn retaining only a life interest in the property. Only two years later, in 1892, Lewis Dillwyn died of a stroke while campaigning for his parliamentary seat at Swansea. As a result Amy was left with no male relative to protect her interests and was compelled to leave Hendrefoilan which had been her home for nearly forty years.

Neither her father's death nor Harry's was completely unexpected since the health of both men had steadily deteriorated during the last few years,

Lewis Dillwyn's through old age and Harry's through excessive drinking. As she had complained to Minnie: 'I doubt whether Papa ages as fast as Harry has done. As you say, men *are* a plague when they will go throwing away their lives, temper, and intellects for liquor! It's generally done through want of something else to do, too.'

Harry's weakness was so generally known in Swansea that the obituary notice in the local press actually referred to his 'Rabelaisian thirst' as one of 'his many and mostly genial eccentricities'. But with all his faults Amy loved him dearly and mourned him deeply. Tall and strongly built, Harry delighted in the outdoor life he and Amy had shared together when they were youngsters at Parkwern and Hendrefoilan. A not very successful member of the south Wales Bar he devoted himself to shooting game and playing at soldiers with the 3rd Glamorgan Rifle Volunteers Corps commanded by his father.

Popular with the men of the Corps he never missed an opportunity of socializing with other ranks and as Quarter Master his favourite injunction was 'Oh, bother the officers – look after the men first!' One of the founders of the National Liberal Club in London, and like his father an ardent Radical, Harry might well have been his father's successor as Swansea's MP, but somehow he never succeeded in getting his political career off the ground. Some of his surviving family letters show him to have been a good-humoured, easy-going and fundamentally weak man who must have found his strong-willed sister Amy a bit of a puzzle, much as he was fond of her and her stern moral virtues which he could not begin to fathom. Writing from his 'filthy den' at Pump Court in the Temple to one of his nephews he said:

> Last I heard of your Aunt Amy she seemed as sweet as an angel half full of pie but then she had seen no one for a fortnight and had just got in a first-rate crop of hay in first-rate condition. She was pretty fit up to last Ascension day when she ran a bit of religious dissipation in the morning and did her usual work in the day with the usual result, i.e. has been more or less seedy ever since.

In his bluff and breezy way Harry thus succeeded in summing up the essence of Amy's life in the period before she lost Hendrefoilan and all that went with it – including the Home Farm at which she had worked long and hard until it became, unlike so many of her father's enterprises, a profitable concern. By the time that he died Lewis Dillwyn, who had spent so much of his life in Parliament, had no clear idea of the state of his business interests and when the truth slowly emerged Amy began to see that she had been left a crippling legacy.

In his will her father had left Amy the residue of his estate which consisted principally of the Llansamlet Spelter Works. If the loss of her home had been the only major sacrifice Amy would not have been too badly off but, on looking through the company accounts and bank papers, she found that the Spelter Works was far from successful and that there was in fact a total deficit of close on £100,000.

The family lawyers had been less than candid about the Dillwyns' true financial position and Amy suspected that her poor father had been hood-winked over a long period by advisers who were only concerned with their own advantage. Because of the complexity of Lewis Dillwyn's affairs the whole of the estate was put into Chancery while his debts were disentangled from his sadly diminished assets. As residuary legatee Amy found herself in the unfortunate position of having inherited a grave liability rather than a going concern, and she was therefore faced with an agonizing dilemma. She could either wash her hands of the responsibility by allowing the Spelter Works to go bankrupt with the loss of over two hundred jobs or she could try to rescue the whole operation. As one might expect, her family pride and self-respect would not permit her to choose the easier option. So she decided to take the extraordinary course of assuming management of the Works herself, taking no profits and using the income from increased productivity and strict economy to pay off her father's many creditors.

Even if she had been an experienced businessman such an undertaking would have been most hazardous, but it was unheard of for a middle-aged spinster of good birth actually to go into the market place and attempt to run a major industrial concern virtually singlehanded. It was not only unheard of, it was positively unladylike. But in that sense Amy was no lady and her reputation in Swansea was already beginning to alarm her more orthodox contemporaries. One small incident will suffice to indicate her scorn for convention and it was one remembered long after it occurred.

She had been in London when her father died in Swansea's Royal Hotel on 19 June 1892 after being taken ill at an election meeting in the Unitarian Chapel in the High Street. Because of Lewis Dillwyn's forty years' service as Member of Parliament it was thought proper that he have a full-scale public funeral. Amy, however, was reluctant to agree since she disliked ostentatious shows of grief and wanted a strictly private ceremony such as her mother had had in 1866. She yielded only after much pressure had been applied and much indignation expressed, and showed her continuing disapproval by attending the service at Sketty Church wearing a heliotrope skirt, a yellow rose at her waist, fawn-coloured bodice, black jacket, and hat trimmed with bunches of flowers. In response to the raised eyebrows she gravely replied that she belonged to the Mourning Reform Society and therefore declined to wear the obligatory sombre raiment of the bereaved. Her motives in joining the Mourning Reform Society were quite clear. She was aware that working-class families were all too often inclined to spend relatively large sums of money on elaborate and costly burial services they could ill afford. The more simple the funeral the less cost was incurred and the money saved could be put to better use. She also knew that the hastily ordered funeral clothes of the better-off were often produced by the sweated labour of women working long hours in abysmal conditions and that, too, she thought indefensible in a civilized society. Devote your resources to the welfare of the living, she argued, and pay less attention to empty forms and ceremonies. Like many Liberals she was a mixture of the utilitarian and the humanitarian but too much of an individual to be stereotyped by any convenient label.

This incident alone did much to confirm her growing reputation as a formidably unusual woman so when it was later announced that she intended to take on the Llansamlet Spelter Works there was a general feeling that here was a woman to be respected if not altogether approved of. The independence of spirit which aroused admiration could also lead to her increasing isolation whenever her strong views clashed head-on with established opinion. Yet at this critical point in her life when she was faced with enormous burdens and stood almost alone it was her independence that gave her the strength of will to fight on. 'I am taking to the Spelter Works and trying hard to learn the management in case they should eventually become mine.' 'Altogether,' she said proudly, 'I am becoming a man of business.'

Frequently in the years before 1892, when her secure world collapsed, she was prone to adopt the weary negativism of 'Le jeu ne vaut pas la chandelle', simply because she had no real role in life or society. Now with virtually no assets and a mass of liabilities she had for the first time in her life to work, to earn her living, and to restore her family's good name. For the first time the game *was* worth the candle; she could actually do something worthwhile, unlike so many of the bored social butterflies by whom she had been surrounded, and it acted as a kind of spiritual and physical release. So few of her contemporaries could ever free themselves from the sheer boredom of doing nothing and having nothing to do except act as decorative appendages to their husbands or dutiful daughters to their parents.

Amy had never lacked the will, the energy, or the intelligence to lead a useful and rewarding life but now she also had the incentive and the opportunity that she needed. Not that the choice was hers to make as far as leaving her home was concerned because, although the mansion itself remained in the family under the terms of Harry's will, the contents had to be sold to help meet the demands of Lewis Dillwyn's many creditors. She had therefore to endure the deeply humiliating experience of seeing every item of her household come under the auctioneer's hammer. In February 1893 a five-day sale was held at Hendrefoilan at which everything, from the superb antique furniture and silver down to the sheets and blankets, was carried off by an army of eager bidders who had travelled to Swansea from all over the country to take advantage of a rare opportunity. With only a few carefully selected possessions and the bare necessities of life Amy moved into modest lodgings at West Cross with no one but her personal maid remaining with her from a whole retinue of servants.

West Cross was at that time a small village just outside Swansea and every morning Amy caught the Mumbles train to travel to her company office in Cambrian Place, then the business centre of a town still enjoying the prosperity of its coal and metallurgical trade. Like any middle-class man of business she worked from 9 till 5 in the office and often travelled up to Llansamlet to check the day-to-day operation of the Spelter Works where she inspected the furnaces and held detailed discussions with her senior employees.

She carefully examined the account books, supervised the international correspondence conducted by her two clerks (neither of whom shared her command of foreign languages), and appointed a Shropshire man called John Corfield as her manager. With this small staff behind her and cutting her own living expenses to a bare minimum she worked relentlessly for four grinding years to put the Works on to a stable footing, until in 1896 she had managed to find enough money to satisfy her father's creditors and thus got out of Chancery the inheritance he had left her. She was now able to purchase back her own estate and become sole owner of the firm. From then onward 'Dillwyn & Co' meant Amy Dillwyn. Unlike any woman of her time she could say proudly, 'I now belong to the Confraternity of Swansea Traders'.

A year later she was in a position to reward her faithful manager Corfield with a partnership. 'He puts in no capital but he fully deserves what I have given him for the way he has worked for me and stuck to me since Papa's death, besides deserving it for himself for his excellence as a manager.'

Without Corfield's help she would have found it difficult to carry on the day-to-day business of management. Although indisputably the driving force behind Dillwyn & Company she still needed to have one person she could trust who had a thorough knowledge of the metallurgical industry and could supervise the workforce on the factory floor. With Amy as director and Corfield as manager the whole enterprise, which had seemed on the point of collapse, was given a new lease of life.

In 1898 she acknowledged that she had some way to go in her uphill struggle by saying: 'I'm still at the same lodgings as before because I have determined to take no profits out of the Spelter Works for myself until I have paid off all Papa's creditors. But it's rather queerly incongruous to me to be paying perhaps £200 to £300 a week to my workmen, and yet living in these small cheap lodgings. However, incongruous or not, it's honest.' Finally and after years of frugality her patience was finally rewarded and as the new century began she was proud to be able to say: 'At the end of last year I finally paid off *all* the remaining creditors on Papa's estate, and now at last the works are really mine and the deeds in my own possession.'

From being a 'limpet' on her sofa at Hendrefoilan she had in a very short time become the embattled chief executive of a factory on which several hundred people depended for their meagre livelihood. Indeed, in her determination to reduce her personal expenses, Amy often chose not to catch the Mumbles train but to walk the four miles between West Cross and Swansea thereby showing the world that she was truly back on her feet in every sense. 'I rejoice', she said, 'in being able to walk well now – no-one who has not been laid up for years as I was can fully understand the joy of being able to lead an active life again.' The need to work had put an end to her invalid status; by having to run a business and carry out all her responsibilities as an employer she had to forget her own weaknesses, real and imagined, and as a result the mysterious illness which had partially crippled her for so many years simply disappeared.

From this time onward the people of Swansea became accustomed to seeing the figure of a spare, bespectacled woman wearing the plainest of short serge skirts with a pocket on each side in which she buried her hands when talking, a short rather mannish jacket, a very plain hat, sporting a simple bunch of violets at her throat and carrying a walking stick or umbrella, and striding out in a thoroughly businesslike manner. Thus did the personality of 'Miss Dillwyn' begin to emerge into the public consciousness of Swansea as one of the town's leading citizens, unique, a little formidable and wholly admirable.

Out of the need to earn a living and economize, and come to terms with a totally new way of life a 'character' was born and as she became better known so did her special characteristics. When she sat at the top table of various functions and coolly lit up her cigar she was breaking a convention that most women regarded as unchallengable: no lady ever smoked in public; in the privacy of her boudoir or drawing-room perhaps, but not openly. The combination of running her own business and smoking cigars made Amy Dillwyn so exceptional that journalists in search of a good story were bound to seize on her as a remarkable example of the 'new woman' in a 'new century'.

The Celebrity

When in 1902 a reporter from the Cardiff *Western Mail* went along to interview Amy in her offices at Albion Chambers in Swansea he began by questioning her about her unique role as a woman industrialist and then went on to ask her about her habit of cigar-smoking which had gained her so much public attention locally. In reply she reminisced quite happily about how she had started to smoke as a youngster at Hendrefoilan with Harry:

> The first time I ever smoked was when I was a naughty little girl; but that was quite surreptitiously and just for once. My brother and I got up at three or four o'clock in the morning because we wanted to capture a certain moth which only flew at that time, and we got hold of a cigar – I'm not sure if it wasn't two – and we smoked it in the fields. I can only remember this – that it was my brother who was ill and not I.

Her father, tolerant almost to the point of indulgence towards all his children, was not in the least put out by her precocious behaviour and actually encouraged his young daughter's spirit of adventure. 'Smoke where you like,' he used to say to her, 'but don't go into men's smoke rooms or your ears may possibly be offended.' So Amy always avoided such places because she never crossed the Rubicon that lay between mere enjoyment and sheer impropriety. Above all she always saw the quiet Quaker-like humour of her own position whenever she did anything that upset the idea of the narrow-minded and the straitlaced. The story was told of how she was once travelling in a railway compartment with a gentleman who was longing to smoke but reluctant to risk the wrath of the awe-inspiring woman who sat opposite him. After some anxious fidgetty moments trying to summon up his courage he timidly appealed to her: 'Do you object – h'm – madam to just a mild cigarette?' And to his astonishment came the cheery reply, 'Not at all sir; smoke on. I'll join you. Will you try one of mine?'

After she had been talking to the *Western Mail* reporter for some time Amy was about to bring the interview to an end when her manager John Corfield brought out a box of cigars from his desk and invited the young journalist to join him in a smoke. 'Try one of these,' interjected Miss

Dillwyn producing her dainty private cigar case out of which she selected a fine old Intimidad. 'Those others are just the office cigars,' she said encouragingly, 'these are rather better and you can smoke and compare.'

The significance of her cigar-smoking was more than quaint eccentricity despite the lasting (but basically superficial) reputation it gave her. It was an outward manifestation of her uniqueness, her desire to be herself no matter what other people might say or think, provided that what she did was fundamentally decent and honest. 'I like to smoke,' she said, 'I find it puts me in a cheerful humour and I can see no objection to it. Let others do as they like. It suits me and it may not suit them. What I do I do openly; I certainly would never consent to doing it in secret.' She saw nothing undignified or odd about the practice which in later years became her personal hallmark, her passport to the select company of notable eccentrics. When she realized that her cigar-smoking had stamped her indelibly as a genuine 'character' she was not above playing up to her audience and thoroughly enjoyed the mild sensation she caused every time she lit up her cigar in public. Since she saw no harm in it she felt no false sense of shame or embarrassment. As she said herself, one of her favourite mottoes was the Spanish 'soy quien soy' (I am who I am) or more prosaically 'take me or leave me, but anyhow that's me'.

The long article which appeared in the *Western Mail* after that interview resulted in Amy's soon becoming a national celebrity. Almost every newspaper and periodical took up her story and within a year 'Miss Dillwyn of Swansea' was renowned the length and breadth of this country and abroad as the woman who had singlehandedly managed a major industrial concern and established herself as a pre-eminent example of what women could do when given the opportunity of proving their worth.

'One of the most remarkable women in Great Britain', wrote the *Western Mail*. 'One of the most original women of the age', echoed the *Pall Mall Gazette*, and many other newspapers took their cue from those journals. Amy Dillwyn's career as successful novelist, *Spectator* reviewer, home-farm bailiff and spelter manufacturer was recognized for the unique achievement it was. In the light of all her other activities her incidental reputation as a cigar-smoker was always secondary to her real significance as an emancipated woman. If she had become instantly famous only for smoking cigars her story would have been a nine-day wonder but the press had also shrewdly paid tribute to her real importance as a pioneer of women's rights. 'She has elected to *work* in this life', was the keynote of all the publicity she received in the press.

So famous did she become that she actually figured in a 1904 cartoon by Bert Thomas in *Ally Sloper*, a popular comic weekly of the period, which showed Amy complete with Gladstone bag and brolly attempting to find a seat on the Paddington train in a compartment already occupied by a couple of prisoners and their police escort. One of the convicts explains to the formidable lady on the platform that she had better try elsewhere: 'Sorry mum, but we're all pinched in 'ere as it is.'

Quite naturally Amy was gratified to realize that she was now rapidly becoming famous, commenting in her journal:

> Just recently the press have rather gone in for taking me up and have been wanting my photograph and putting in notices about me (and two of the applications came from America). It's very funny because I don't feel as if I was particularly different from other people, as far as *they* can see – tho' in matters that they *don't* see or know about I have an 'inner consciousness' that I am probably somewhat different from the majority.

One of the matters other people certainly did not know about was the reason why she had become a businesswoman in the first place. Nobody knew how close the spelter works had come to bankruptcy and how hard Amy had been compelled to work to save the firm from insolvency and the Dillwyns from losing their good name as reputable employers. The public at large immediately recognized her courage and initiative but had no idea of the magnitude of the task she had undertaken and the frightening risk of failure. Nor did they know anything about the private hardships and the personal rebuffs she had to endure on her way to becoming a celebrated figure.

When she lost her brother and father in quick succession Amy could have turned to several wealthy relatives for support and she regarded with deep gratitude the generous offers of help she had received from her cousin Sir John Talbot Dillwyn Llewelyn when the crisis came. Sir John, the son of her distinguished uncle John Dillwyn Llewelyn, was a country squire who lived in considerable style at Penllergaer a large estate just outside Swansea. He and his equally distinguished wife Lady Julia (who was the sister of Sir Michael Hicks-Beach, twice Chancellor of the Exchequer) always welcomed Amy as one of the family and were the souls of kindness when she had literally nowhere else to turn. 'Penllergaer has been like a second home to me since I lost Hendrefoilan,' she acknowledged gratefully, but she would not seek charity even from those able and willing to offer it. She had made up her mind to find her own salvation through work and work she did, however many daunting setbacks she had to suffer.

In view of Sir John's sympathetic attitude it seemed ironic that her own sister Minnie, far from helping her, in fact caused her further anxiety by disputing the division of some of their father's property. In the course of this dispute she sent Minnie a gentle reprimand that epitomized her delicacy and dignity in everything that touched her self-respect. Minnie had complained because Amy had sold off some family sketches without consulting her and she replied with a quiet reproach to her sister and nephew:

> I think you will see that if I had so consulted you before coming to such a decision it would have been simply out of pure 'pity and fullness of heart' – to use the words John employed in writing to *me* at the time when he and you accused me of *asking* for charity. And, as I have already told you, your accusing me of this left me no possible means of clearing myself of the charge save to show that I had an equivalent to offer in *return* for what I asked; consequently I did not consult you as to what I should do. No one can regret more than I do that this unpleasantness has arisen between us, but it wasn't I who began it. My original intention was to give you freely any sketches that you wished for, if ever they came to me as residuary legatee, and I think that shows you how entirely I had been prepared to act in accordance with the strong sisterly love that you and I have always borne each other. Your loving sister, E.A. Dillwyn.

Such a letter written by a middle-aged spinster who had lost everything she cherished to a comfortably-married sister whose eldest son John was about to take possession of Hendrefoilan is striking testimony to Amy's sense of decency and honour, the Christian virtues she practised as sincerely as she preached. But the pill was no less bitter for all that.

Amy showed the same kind of love and forgiveness to her younger sister when, just six months after her disagreement with Minnie, she received an urgent message from Essie that she was gravely ill and alone in Coventry where she had been appearing with a company of strolling players. Follow-ing her elopement with Richard Pakenham Essie had completely cut herself off from her family, and had not even attended her father's funeral. Yet in this crisis it was to Amy that she turned first. Caring and conscientious as ever Amy hurried off to comfort Essie and found her in considerable distress in bleak lodgings with no sign of Richard Pakenham. Scorning any temptation to preach a sermon and say 'I told you so', Amy called in nurses and did all she could to fight for Essie's recovery. But within a fortnight Essie was dead and Amy had to return to Swansea to continue her own struggle for survival.

Behind the indomitable face she showed the outside world there were times when she was truly desolate and on one page of her diary, smudged by what might well have been her own tears, she wrote on her forty-ninth birthday a heart-rending confession:

> For the first time in my life my birthday has passed without one single greeting. Papa and Harry used always to remember the day and Minnie always wrote a 'many happy returns of the day' letter. But this year no living soul has remembered – it makes me feel terribly solitary in the world. Perhaps when one's as lonely as this a wish of 'returns of the day' would be necessarily a farce.

But with the responsibilities of being a hard-working industrialist Amy did not have time to indulge in prolonged spells of self-pity nor had she ever failed to bounce back after being hurt and lonely. When her rare moments of gloom had passed she found that her new mobility had opened up all kinds of possibilities she would never have previously contemplated. She took up hockey and founded a team of twenty men and twenty women called 'the Dillwyn Hockey Club' which played regular matches on the cricket field in the grounds of the Vivian mansion at Singleton. Always a keen swimmer in her youth she started to play water polo enthusiastically in middle-age and became so proficient she was able to play competitively. When she needed to relax from her more strenuous activities she hired a boat and spent a whole day fishing and bathing off the Mumbles often in the company of her young nephews and nieces. It was tremendous fun for people half her age to visit this exuberant woman who eagerly joined in their games and make-believe and left them all behind in her youthful vitality for whatever prank caught her imagination.

One of the most heartening results of her becoming solvent was that in 1902 she could afford to move out of her 'small cheap lodgings' and take a yearly tenancy on a little house in West Cross which she called 'Cadlys' using the Welsh word for camp because it was only a temporary residence till her finances improved. Nothing could better illustrate how far down the social scale she had fallen when her father died (and how far she had recovered) than her deep sense of personal satisfaction at having her own belongings around her again rather than other people's:

> I moved in on 3rd October and for the first time for ten years I slept in my *own* bed, with my *own* sheets and my *own* blankets. I have had to furnish the tiny place and feel just like a child playing with a doll's house.

Two years later the works had prospered sufficiently to allow her to leave her 'doll's house' and buy a more substantial property called Tŷ Glyn just off the busy Mumbles Road, which was to be her home for the remainder of her life.

So from the dark days of 1892 when she seemed to have lost everything and had even been accused of asking for charity by her nearest relatives Amy had pulled herself up to a position where she had turned a bankrupt enterprise into a profitable concern, paid off the huge burden of her father's accumulated debts, achieved national celebrity and, best of all, become the owner of her own home at West Cross. After a decade of struggle and hardship she was finally independent and free.

Grand Old Lady

Now that she was again a woman of substance and had for the first time the ability to control her own life Amy was in a position where she could look to the future with some confidence. Ten years earlier she had been only too glad simply to survive and save the family name from the stigma of failure, but having rescued the Dillwyns she realized more keenly than ever that she was the last to bear the name which meant so much to her.

The Dillwyn family had been established in Swansea as far back as 1802 with the arrival from London of her grandfather Lewis Weston Dillwyn and for nearly a century the Dillwyns had been one of the most prominent families in south Wales. As owners of the Cambrian Pottery, as Members of Parliament for Swansea, as leading local industrialists and magistrates, they had made a major contribution to every aspect of the cultural, social and economic life of the area, and now Amy was deeply concerned that after the death of her brother Harry there was no longer a male heir to continue the line.

She looked therefore to her sister's youngest son Rice Nicholl of Merthyr Mawr as her successor both in the family and the firm. When Rice married Harriet Gilbertson the daughter of a Pontardawe industrialist in 1904 Amy asked him to take the name of Dillwyn and join her as a director of Dillwyn & Co. When he accepted her offer she said: 'My father left me his heir, and I think it is one of the duties of an heir to try and carry on the name so that is my reason for asking Rice to take it. Up to then I was the sole living person of the name I believe. So there is once more a Mr Dillwyn.'

The first task of the new 'Mr Dillwyn' was to learn about the business his aunt intended to leave him. Her Dillwyn Spelter Works was one of the largest producers of zinc in the United Kingdom and although she had managed, almost miraculously, to turn its heavy losses into a reasonable profit of about £10,000 per annum there were still substantial problems to be tackled. One of the major difficulties that faced the small independent zinc producers at this period was finding suitable high-grade ores for the spelter processing. The big German and American companies had the financial means to explore and exploit mineral resources all over the world but the independents were obliged to look for whatever suppliers they could afford to come to terms with. Algeria was one of the smaller exporters of zinc ore (calamine) and in 1905 Amy saw an opportunity of opening up a new source of raw material which would keep her Llansamlet works in business in the face of increasingly ruthless competition from abroad.

She also saw that here was an opportunity to introduce Rice Dillwyn to the mysteries of commerce so, just a few weeks after his marriage, she invited him to join her on an exploratory trip to Algeria. With extraordinary pluck and stamina she travelled with Rice and a small party of technical advisers through the wild snow-clad scenery of the Atlas Mountains riding astride mules (since there were no ladylike side-saddles) and actually going down the mines to inspect the seams of ore before comitting herself to any contracts. Few male entrepreneurs of the period would have been so diligent in their explorations and for a woman to be so involved was unheard of. Quite unperturbed by the harsh weather and isolated terrain, but admitting that she was perished with cold and had not changed her clothes for a week at a time, Amy joined her male companions in all the technical discussions and financial bargaining that ensued and was happy to end the day with a game of bridge or poker. Rice Dillwyn quickly learnt what it meant to be a working industrialist.

When they returned to Wales from Algeria Amy was surprised to find waiting for her an offer that she could not refuse. The powerful German metallurgical company Metallgesellschaft of Frankfurt was busily buying up independent zinc producers as an outlet for their vast reserves of zinc ores and since Amy realized that a merger with such an industrial giant could only benefit Dillwyn & Co. she accepted their offer for her majority shareholding. She was shrewd enough to see that in the twentieth century there was no long-term future for small specialist firms and that the British zinc industry was already in decline *vis-à-vis* its great American and German competitors. Ensuring that Rice Dillwyn kept his place on the board she kept only a nominal shareholding for herself and withdrew from her active role as managing director. The extent of her personal involvement in the day-to-day running of the whole enterprise became clear when the time came to retire and lay down the responsibilities that she had come to take in her stride and even to enjoy:

I am now a mere insignificant shareholder, having nothing more to do with shaping and controlling the business. I didn't like giving it up and wouldn't have done so if I hadn't felt bound to look first at the interests of the company before my own inclinations. I felt it was best for my beloved Dillwyn & Co to agree to the proposal of Metallgesellschaft that I sell them the bulk of my shares at market price. They have a very large control of zinc ore and wanted to get a finger into a zinc smelting business. We on the other hand are always hunting about for zinc ore and a junction between them and us ensures a supply of ore for many years to come.

No longer having her office and factory to attend to every day of the week and with Dillwyn & Co. reasonably secure for the foreseeable future Amy was able to give more attention to the public life of Swansea. She had already sat on various charitable boards and friendly societies and now had the leisure to devote herself to active service on behalf of a town which looked to her for leadership and initiative as a woman with a substantial stake in the community.

She stood for the Swansea School Board, was elected near the top of the poll against twenty other candidates, and immediately became Chairman of the Truant School Committee which she then transformed into a more constructive body called the Industrial School whose objective was to train the truants for useful careers in industry. When the 1902 Education Act put an end to School Boards the local authority became responsible for education in Swansea and wanted Amy to become a co-opted member. Independent as ever she declined to 'be thrust down the ratepayers' throats without their being able to get rid of me if they wish' and did not accept. When she lost elections she did not seek appointment by the back door.

Her particular interest lay in the care of the sick and she devoted a great deal of time and energy to her work on the Hospital Management Committee of which she was made President in 1901. She had long recognized the town's need for a convalescent home to supplement the work of the General Hospital which had been built by public subscription some thirty years earlier, but she also realized that such an undertaking would require a very substantial outlay to meet both the capital expenditure and cover the running costs. Amy herself lacked the funds for such a project so she privately approached her old friend Clara Thomas of Llwynmadoc (Llewellyn Thomas's sister) and asked for her support. Clara Thomas, an immensely rich and philanthropic spinster who had already disbursed a small fortune on similar charitable works, agreed to endow the princely sum of £10,500 on condition that her donation remained anonymous. Amy then set to work to raise a further £4,000 towards the cost of buying the site and erecting the buildings and by the summer of 1903 the new Convalescent Home situated in a beautiful area overlooking Cwmdonkin Park was ready to open its doors. Amy proudly accepted the tributes of a grateful Swansea to 'X' the mysterious benefactor. By one of life's little ironies Clara had inherited the enormous wealth of Llwynmadoc as a direct result of the untimely death of her only brother Llewellyn. Had Amy's engagement to Llewellyn ended in marriage rather than tragedy, the largesse she was distributing on Clara's behalf would have been her own.

As a result of her dedication to the Convalescent Home Amy naturally expected a little consideration from her colleagues on the Hospital Board but found that they treated her with bureaucratic clumsiness. In a meeting to discuss the appointment of new trustees some of Amy's opponents insisted on an election which led to her being outvoted. Deeply hurt she stalked out of the committee room and vowed never to be humiliated again, however good the cause she had espoused. Her supporters at once came to her defence pointing out in heated correspondence in the newspapers that few people had done so much, so selflessly for their native town. A letter from Fred Rocke a local woollen merchant was typical of the kind of loyalty she inspired among those who recognized her dogged sense of duty:

> If there is an institution in the town where a capable, energetic, able, live, fearless woman is wanted, it is at our hospital. Miss Dillwyn has all these qualifications and with them she has a woman's heart, full of love and sympathy for the poor, afflicted and helpless. She did her work there because she loved it. I do hope that, notwithstanding all that has happened, Miss Dillwyn will see her way in the interest of the poor and suffering to continue this noble and unselfish work which she has done so ably in the past.

Her concern for the underdog surfaced again in the winter of 1911 when she played an active role in a highly controversial strike by twenty-five women employees of Ben Evans, the great emporium which had dominated Swansea's central shopping area for many years. As part of the growing movement for better pay and conditions in the years just before the First World War the dressmakers at Ben Evans had taken the almost unprecedented step of striking for a living wage. Such a demand obviously caused consternation among the local shopkeepers, many of whom had formerly been the mainstay of her father's political support, but Amy saw the issue as a simple manifestation of the right to receive a decent wage for long hours of sweated labour. She called for an immediate boycott of the store until the dressmakers' grievances had been rectified and asked her own family and friends to withdraw their custom.

Mass demonstrations of five or six thousand people were held in Swansea in support of 'the Ben Evans girls' and Amy was invited to take the chair at a large meeting addressed by prominent public figures like Mary McArthur and Margaret Bondfield who had come to help organize the newly-formed branch of the National Federation of Women Workers. The local press reported her as saying that justice had to be done:

> Employers have no right to avail themselves of the necessities of poor people, to grind them down to take unfair wages or to make them accept unfair conditions of labour. Is five shillings a living wage? ('No.') If twenty girls had an increase of two shillings a week it would mean a lot to them, and if the proposals were put to the store's shareholders they would say, I feel sure, 'Let the girls have it by all means.' ('Cheers') I always make it a rule never to deal with a firm in which I know conditions of work and wages are bad and at present I cannot see my way to deal with Messrs Ben Evans and I hope everyone else will feel likewise.

Looking at the plight of the dressmakers Amy saw quite clearly that the women were in a sense worse off than their menfolk, because the men at least had a union and a parliamentary vote with which they could influence their working conditions. The women had nothing but public sympathy to support them. She recalled that when she herself had been a large employer of labour she had paid out wages every week to nearly three hundred men who all enjoyed a right to vote which was denied to her. The cause of the Ben Evans girls was very near to the heart of someone who knew exactly what it felt like to be a mere woman with no man to defend her interests in an intensely competitive world. As she said on many an occasion, she deserved a vote as much as her workmen and could exercise it just as intelligently.

She was fully aware of the prejudice against women in public life from her experience as a candidate in various non-parliamentary elections. She stood for the influential Swansea Harbour Trust in 1903 and for the newly-constituted Swansea County Council in 1907 and had each time been defeated by the entrenched bias against female interlopers into a strictly male preserve, however distinguished their record of public service. As the *Cambrian Daily Leader* noted when she lost the Harbour Trust election:

> Criticism of Miss Dillwyn is summed up in a single sentence. She is a woman, not a man. The sex disability is, however, so real that her

recognised administrative ability and freedom from the feminine idio-
syncracies which might prove embarrassing at gatherings of businessmen
failed to remove it.

When the National Union of Women's Suffrage Societies was formed at
the turn of the century Amy was among its earliest supporters in south
Wales, and never wavered in her fight for female emancipation. She could
not, however, ally herself with the militant suffragette movement led by
Mrs Emmeline Pankhurst and her daughters because she would not counte-
nance violent methods as a means of winning the franchise. Invariably she
took the common-sense view: 'All I say is, give women a chance. Don't
despise them without knowing what they can do. A woman's duty, like a
man's, is to serve her generation in the way she can do it best.'

In 1914 the women of Great Britain showed how right Amy and the
suffragists were. As the men flocked to the trenches the women filled the
vacant places in a way that would have been impossible in peacetime. They
manned the trams and buses, the shipyards and the foundries, and especially
the vital munitions factories, contributing an unprecedented share of the
national workload and in so doing revolutionized their own place in society.
By the end of the war they had not only gained the vote but changed their
own and their daughters' future. They were no longer compelled to be
either dolls or drudges. For the first time in history they had played their full
part in their country's survival. As a result things would never be quite the
same again however many inequalities remained to be ironed out in the rest
of the twentieth century. Amy was by then seventy and too old to take an
active role in the war effort. She could only look on as several of her nephews and great nephews died in the carnage of France and Belgium. But even
she was not totally unaffected by the enormity of the sacrifice when in 1916
she watched the first Zeppelin raid over London and saw bombs being
dropped not far from her club. In the following year she was again in
London in the middle of an air raid that lasted seven days on end, but she
refused to be frightened by the destruction all around her:

At my club we played bridge through the bombing until the lights had
to be put out and then we went to the ground floor and smoked and
talked until the lights were turned on again. I was at the theatre one
night and the play went on as usual in spite of the noise of guns and
about ten o'clock Dion Boucicault announced that the 'All Clear' had
been signalled.

When the final 'All Clear' sounded with the signing of the Armistice in November 1918 Amy looked out on a world that had changed beyond recognition. Many of the most promising young men of the Edwardian period had fallen on the battlefields, women had largely come into their own, and the economic structure of the nation had been severely dislocated. So far as the Works was concerned times became bleak. The exceptional rise in demand for zinc as part of the war effort had faded rapidly and the Americans were in a position to monopolize the world market. By 1922 the Llansamlet Spelter operation was forced to shut down temporarily and by the time of the General Strike of 1926 had closed altogether, ending a Dillwyn connection that had lasted for nearly seventy years.

Always a realist, Amy accepted that the world had moved on and that not even her beloved Dillwyn & Co. could last for ever. She was nevertheless pleased when in 1923 one of Swansea's leading young businessmen, John Oliver Watkins, asked her if she would allow her name to be used in the title of a new building society, and for the next sixty years the Dillwyn Permanent Building Society remained as a public tribute to a woman who had become almost an institution in her own lifetime. As she grew older Amy was perfectly happy to accept a stream of invitations to address meetings, open bazaars, lay foundation stones, review the local militia, and generally lend her support to every kind of event that sought her patronage as Swansea's first lady.

Her exceptionally active public life was also complemented by an equally rewarding private life which took her on many holidays abroad to all kinds of interesting places. In the winter of 1920 when she was seventy-five she was glimpsed by a reporter on the *Menton and Monte Carlo News* savouring the delights of high society on the Riviera in the company of such fashionable notabilities as Lily Langtry's husband, Sir Hugo de Bathe:

> Another interesting personality seen for a moment on her way to the baccarat room was Miss Dillwyn. In her tailor-made clothes, silk in the evening, cloth in the day, with stiff collars and cuffs and old fashioned jewelry she sits up with the best playing bridge or poker or anything that happens. Over seventy but very sporting, she smokes small cigars and wears panama or felt hats of a mannish build, wholly oblivious of the interest she excites especially among foreigners. She is to be seen all over the place, calm and unconcerned but wholly delightful. It is refreshing to meet elderly women of this sort, and so rare.

Rare indeed and rarer than he knew because few people at Monte Carlo in 1920 could have guessed the story behind the delightful elderly woman sitting at the baccarat table who had made her debut into London's fashionable society more than half a century before and who was destined to survive as Swansea's 'grand old lady' for another fifteen years.

Epilogue

Amy Dillwayn died peacefully at Tŷ Glyn just before Christmas 1935. She had been ill for only a few days and passed away six months after her ninetieth birthday. In accordance with her strongly held views on burial and family mourning her remains were cremated at Pontypridd with no ostentatious ceremony of any kind and her ashes were laid to rest in the Dillwyn grave almost opposite the north door of Sketty Church alongside her parents and her beloved brother Harry.

The local papers marked her passing by publishing long articles filled with respectful admiration for all her sterling qualities, paying warm tribute to her remarkable achievement as a businesswoman whose long career was without parallel not only in her native Wales but in the whole country. Her distinctive personality, deliberately cultivated in the closing period of her life, had perhaps inevitably set her apart from a general public which saw her as a formidable old lady slightly larger than life who did not suffer fools gladly, never courted easy popularity, and was not amenable to social flattery. They saw her riding around Swansea in her pony and trap and later, when her finances improved, in her chauffeur-driven car and they naturally looked up to her as a 'grand old lady' who had worked unstintingly for her fellow citizens even if they found it hard to fathom her quite exceptional character. Her relatives, close friends and servants on the other hand, while fully aware of the unorthodox aspects of her personality, were also more conscious of her loyalty, her devotion to their interests, and the loving nature she had never been fully able to express.

She had made her will some three years previously and when it was proved in the Carmarthen district probate registry early in 1936 the change in her fortunes became dramatically clear. Her father's debts when he died in 1892 had amounted to over £100,000 largely due to the mismanagement of his various business enterprises. Yet Amy's will revealed that her estate had been sworn to the value of over £114,000, mainly the result of her sale of Dillwyn & Co. to the giant firm of Metallgesellschaft at Frankfurt. So the wheel had come full circle – from apparent prosperity through financial disaster and back again to real wealth created by her own business acumen and the gruelling labour of her employees at Llansamlet.

The bulk of her estate she left to her favourite nephew Rice Mansel Dill-wyn who was also her executor but she also left substantial sums to other relatives including Oonagh Pakenham, Essie's daughter by her second marriage to the actor Richard Pakenham. Nor did she forget the loyalty of her domestic staff, leaving extremely generous legacies to her personal maid Maggie Warren, her parlour maid Martha Davies, and her faithful chauffeur Trevor Bond who had proudly driven her around Swansea and South Wales in great style after she had established her position as a woman of substance. No one who might have been aware of her catastrophic situation in 1892 could have dreamt that this embattled woman would emerge forty years later as a very rich and highly-respected local dowager. She had fought and won a tremendous battle but at what cost? Never one to parade her private feelings even to her own family she must often have felt that despite her eventual affluence her life had lacked many of the rewards and pleasures that women of her class and background would normally have expected and enjoyed. She had lived largely alone and died with few close relatives and friends near at hand and her material success, however gratifying her sense of achievement, could perhaps never compensate her for all she lost when her fiancé died.

Her elder sister Mary De la Beche Nicholl, her 'dearest Minnie', had died peacefully at Merthyr Mawr in 1922 after leading a life so unusual that she has her own biography in Hilary Thomas's *Grandmother Extraordinary*, and her mansion at Merthyr Mawr remains the home of the descendants of the Nicholl family. As for the rest of Amy's family history her nephew and sole heir Rice Mansel Dillwyn had only one son, Colin, whom Amy fondly anticipated would continue the Dillwyn tradition through the twentieth century and beyond. After a distinguished academic career at Oxford where he became a tutor at Christ Church, Colin Dillwyn volunteered for military service just before the outbreak of the Second World War and in May 1940 found himself cut off with the British Expeditionary Force trying to reach the beaches of Dunkirk. The young lieutenant was killed by German tank-fire while shielding two of his comrades who still remember his great gallantry. If Amy had survived a few years longer she would thus have experienced yet another family tragedy, even though she would have been immensely proud to know that Colin Dillwyn had shown the same kind of dedication and self-sacrifice in his short life that she, in her own way, had shown throughout hers.

So Rice Nicholl's change of surname proved in the end to have been fruitless. Although he lived on until 1959 the loss of his only son meant that the male line had again come to an end, leaving the Dillwyn ideals to be sustained by his surviving daughters, one of whom, Olga Welbourn, has handed on the story of her great-aunt Amy to the present generation in the form of the diaries and letters from which this narrative has been written. Without Olga Welbourn's help the biography of Amy Dillwyn would never have been possible, although she bears no responsibility for the way in which the tale has been told.

Of the fine houses that Amy knew some are gone but several still remain much as she would have remembered them. Her birthplace at Parkwern, much altered and extended, is now the Swansea Nurses' Home at Park Beck – a transformation that she with her lifelong interest in caring for the sick would have appreciated. Hendrefoilan House, where she grew up and which she lost so unexpectedly, afterwards came into the hands of another Swansea industrialist Sir John Bryn Edwards whose wife Kathleen was, by a strange quirk of fate, the daughter of Amy's loyal works manager at Llansamlet, John Corfield. When the Edwards family sold the Hendrefoilan estate in 1964 the mansion was bought by the University College of Swansea for use as its education centre while parts of the extensive grounds and gardens are now a modern housing development.

The Dillwyn Spelter Works at Llansamlet fell into a steady decline when the demand for zinc was drastically curtailed after the First World War, finally closing down altogether during the industrial depression in 1926. The ruins stood as a grim monument to Swansea's former metallurgical supremacy until they were eventually demolished by the Royal Engineers on a weekend exercise in 1962 as part of the campaign to clean up the awful dereliction of the Lower Swansea Valley. The impressive eighteenth-century mansion of Sketty Hall, where Amy used to visit her much loved grandfather Lewis Weston Dillwyn, has for many years been a major centre of technological research, carrying on at a modern professional level the amateur scientific skills of the Dillwyn family. And just across the park from Sketty Hall stands Singleton Abbey, once the splendid home of the Dillwyns' perennial rivals the Vivians and now the administrative centre of the University College of Swansea.

Margam Castle, where Amy regularly enjoyed the palatial lifestyle of her friends Emily, Bertha and Olive Talbot, suffered long years of neglect and became semi-derelict but the surrounding estate and the great Orangery have now been taken over and restored by the West Glamorgan Country Council as a country park devoted to the leisure of the public at large. Penllergaer, too, where Amy received so much hospitality when she most needed it, is planned as a leisure area but the house itself was demolished in 1961 and is now the site of the Lliw Valley District Council headquarters. Amy's last and most satisfying home, Tŷ Glyn, is still a private residence. She and her family lie in Sketty churchyard only a few feet away from the grave of her assiduous suitor the Reverend Edward Bolney. Parson Bolney (afterwards misnamed Bonley in Francis Kilvert's famous diaries) kept his promise never to marry and served Sketty as a devoted and faithful parish priest for over half a century until his death in 1906. The village of Killay whose social and religious life caused Amy so much heart-searching has since grown into a pleasant and thriving suburb of Swansea and still retains much of its old village atmosphere (including its Commercial Inn), even if it shows hardly a trace of the 'uproarious conditions' she so vividly described.

Although the Dillwyns have now vanished as a family they live on in Swansea and the surrounding area in names like Dillwyn Street and Dillwyn Road, Lewis Street and Llewelyn Street, and in De la Beche Road and De la Beche Street. As long as the streets survive so will the memory of the family which did so much to shape the pattern of Swansea's history in the nineteenth century and long after. And of that extraordinary family it is Amy Dillwyn who lives longest and most clearly in recollections of the old town and its people.

Index

Gladstone, Catherine 51
Gladstone, William 50–1
Glamorgan Pottery 11, 15
Glamorgan Rifle Volunteer Corps 58, 70
Gilbertson, Harriet 82
Goss, Sir John 52–3
Grandmother Extraordinary 91

Haynes, George 5
Helena, Princess 1
Hendrefoilan *passim*
Heneage, Major Clement, V.C. 35
Herbert, Auberon 51, 54
Hesse, Prince and Princess Louis of 22, 50
Hewson, Revd William 10
Hicks-Beach family 59
Hicks-Beach, Lady Julia 78
Home Farm (Hendrefoilan) 70
Howells, William Dean 66
Hughes, Thomas 51
Hutton, Richard Holt 64

Industrial School, Swansea 84

Jamaica 8, 10
Jill 63
Jill and Jack 63–4

Kaiser Wilhelm II, of Prussia 1
Keevil, Wilts. 8
Killay 24, 30, 32, 42, 43–8, 49, 54, 59, 62, 93

Lewis, Sally 36
Lilliput, Swansea 9–10

Llansamlet Spelter Works, 71–74, 78, 82, 88, 92
Llewelyn, Colonel John 93
Llewelyn, John Dillwyn 5, 8, 10, 14, 18, 24, 30, 62
Llewelyn, Sir John Talbot Dillwyn 78
Llewelyn, Elinor 25

Llewelyn, Emma (later Crichton) 30
Llewelyn, Lucy 25
Llewelyn, Mary (*see* Adams)
Llewelyn, Thereza (later Story Maskelyne) 31
Llwynmadoc 22, 25
Lorne, Marquis of 50
Louise, Princess 50

Margam Castle 19, 23, 29, 32, 34, 42, 92
Merthyr Mawr 18, 23, 27, 40
Metallgesellschaft (Frankfurt) 83
Middlemarch 61
Mill, John Stuart 54
Moggridge, Weston 41, 54
Monte Carlo 89
Mourning Reform Society 72
Mumbles 80
Mumbles train 73

National Federation of Women Workers 86
National Union of Women's Suffrage Societies 87
Nicholl, Sir John 18
Nicholl, John Cole (Johnny) 18–19, 23–4, 27
Nicholl, John Iltyd Dillwyn 69
Nicholl, Rice (afterwards Dillwyn) 97–8, 82–3, 91
Nightingale, Florence 53, 60

Oystermouth Church 54

Paget, Lady Florence 28
Pakenham, Richard 68, 79
Pall Mall Gazette 77
Pankhurst, Emmeline 87
Parkwern 12–14, 35, 36, 92
Penllergaer 5, 8, 10, 18, 24, 27, 30–31, 62, 78, 92
Penrice 18
Pontarddulais 14
Pusey, Edward 54